TIM KEY

CHAPTERS.

www.utterandpress.co.uk
ISBN: 978-1-9162226-8-7

TO

MARLOW JUNIPER SHARPE

CONTENTS.

HALFWAY.

★ KEY: Well, here it is, Em.

JUNIPER: "Chapter One".

KEY: I can't get over your hair.

JUNIPER: Well, you're gonna have to try.

KEY: Of course I'm trying, Em.

JUNIPER: This place is *nice!*

KEY: Well, what did you expect? You want us to squat in a recycling plant? Sipping discarded Hoegaardens, going through the poems?

JUNIPER: Well, I dunno, do I?

KEY: We're not savages, Em.

JUNIPER: Are we getting drinks?

KEY: Drinks, food. Read the poems. A lush afternoon, basically.

JUNIPER: Heaven.

KEY: Look, I'll get the waiter-guy's attention.

JUNIPER: So, what are you giving me here?

KEY: It's chapter one. We'll go through them one by one, I thought.

JUNIPER: A little bundle of poems.

KEY: Right. To get us started. *Sir!*

JUNIPER: Well, don't click your fingers.

KEY: Well, what do you want me to click?

JUNIPER: Don't click anything.

KEY: Well, I've clicked 'em now, haven't I?

JUNIPER: "Chapter One". Oh. "A Real Friend". Little titles for all the poems.

KEY: Where d'ya get it done, anyway?

JUNIPER: Huh?

KEY: The mop, Em. The mop!

JUNIPER: Blummell did it.

KEY: Dear old Blummell.

JUNIPER: We got lashed and cut each other's hair.

KEY: Well, if it's any consolation, it doesn't look like the stylings of a drunk.

JUNIPER: I'll tell her that. Stop clicking, can ya!

KEY: Yes, hello, sir. Can we get a Beck's Vier please –

JUNIPER: Sorry about his clicking stuff, he's based in London –

KEY: And a gin and peppermint, for my friend, dear sir.

JUNIPER: Hell yeah!

KEY: I've written a book of poems.

JUNIPER: He doesn't need to know that, Tim.

KEY: And she's designing them.

JUNIPER: I design all his poems. We're a team.

CHAPTER ONE.*

*JUNIPER: The first poem.
  KEY: Get it out of the way.
  JUNIPER: I like it.
  KEY: Not about that, Em. Just get it down. Get your feet under the table, that's all.
  JUNIPER: Who's the friend?
  KEY: Let's not analyse the first one, Em.
  JUNIPER: Well, I'm all for it.
  KEY: Thank God for that.
  JUNIPER: They're my kind of thing, that's all.
  KEY: I'm happy you like it.
  JUNIPER: I sometimes think I'm crazy.
  KEY: Oh, okay.

A REAL FRIEND.*

My friend agreed to meet me and drink beer with me.
It was exhilarating.
We had what you might call "a shorthand".
It was so fucking *sparky*.
We ordered crisps.
Ultimately, conversation ran dry.
I accused him of being "sour".
He brought up some crap that happened, what, fifteen years ago.
Fucking pointless.
I gave him a dead leg, he deleted me from his phone, I put my heel through his bollocks.
I gave him a missed call later and he texted back.
He sent me emojis, I sent him kisses.
We built bridges.
I thanked him for coming to the pub.
We agreed to meet that night for a couple.

Chapter One

HOME OFFICE.

I came home and there was a receptionist in my flat.
"Yes, can I help you, sir?"
She'd set up in the hall bit and had a Dell laptop and *a phone headset* on.
"Can I help you?" she said again.
"I live here," I muttered.
I was keeping my cool, but I was pretty much not on board with all this.
"Can I get past, please?" She was right in my way; her bloody great swivel chair was pressed up against my shoe-rack.
"Can I take your name, sir?"
What was she going on about?
She had a blouse and a little name badge which said "Chapman" on it.
"Who are you here to see?"
"Myself!" I was starting to shake; what in the hell was going on here?
She had a packed lunch box on her desk; I could identify a stinking mousse through its partially translucent lid.
"How do you mean 'yourself', I'm sorry?"
I bowed my head, snarled into my tie.
I thought I could hear someone doing a presentation in my bedroom.

MEAL DEAL.*

The chap in Pret said he'd give me my mocha for free if I
gave his boss a dead arm and called him a twerp.
I said I'd do no such thing, I'd be happy to pay.
He said he'd throw in a banana *and* a carrot cake.
I looked at the smoothies and he told me that that stuff
wasn't part of the deal.
I bit my lip.
"Which one's your boss?"
His eyeballs twitched towards a thin, bald fellow and I slid
my Barclays Premier card back into my shirt pocket.

---

*JUNIPER: You always talk about Pret.
KEY: Okay.

WEB.*

Mike walked into a cobweb.
He stuck to it and a spider obviously took an interest in him.
The spider eventually covered Mike with a weird chemical
excreted from her eyes and that is the current state of play.
That is where we are now.
Mike trapped.
His missus on her way home on the bus.

---

*JUNIPER: Does he get out?
KEY: Don't know, doesn't say.
JUNIPER: I know, but… it's your poem.
KEY: But… yeah. But I don't know if he gets out.
JUNIPER: I bet he does.
KEY: You'd think he can sort it. Or else his wife can.
JUNIPER: She can use scissors or secateurs.
KEY: It doesn't say how big the spider is, that's the only thing.
JUNIPER: Well, you invented her.
KEY: I have no idea how big she is.
JUNIPER: You must have a notion.
KEY: Size of a tortoise, maybe.
JUNIPER: Oh, okay. Christ, it could go either way.
KEY: Sort of depends how far away the bus is, Em.

MY FELLOW MAN.*

I was people-watching.
Sat with my hot drinkie, gawping outta the window at
Starbucks.
My goodness, what a shower: these people!
Shoddily dressed, dragging their feet, spitting and honking,
what a fucking society.
I hammered on the window.
"Hey you guys! I'm trying to people-watch here. Buck your
fucking ideas up! Gimme something to watch!"
A few threw their shoulders back, became more animated,
looked a bit more into it.
One guy took his top off.
That was a bit more like it.

---

*JUNIPER: Scrutinising your fellow man.
   KEY: That's the idea.
   JUNIPER: They're not there for your entertainment, yer know.
   KEY: But in the fifties, I bet –
   JUNIPER: But we're not living in the fifties.
   KEY: I can only imagine how nice that would have been. All those men in suits.
   JUNIPER: And nicely dressed women.
   KEY: Tell me about it.
   JUNIPER: A bygone era.
   KEY: Now all we seem to get is these… Neanderthals. Dragging their knuckles,
      anoraks hanging off their shoulders, clutching beaten-up A-Zs, crack
      pipes clinking on the pavement.
   JUNIPER: Did they have bowler hats in the fifties, do we think?
   KEY: I bet they did, Em. I bet you couldn't fucking move for 'em.

SAUSAGES.*

Some poor bastard got buried alive.

He texted everyone in his phone.

But his thumbs had gone fat through lack of oxygen and, unfortunately, it was a case of typos galore.

He wrote "Boris" instead of "buried", for example, and "he he" instead of "help!"

So people either didn't reply or else they did reply but they replied saying he was talking a load of old shit.

---

* **KEY:** What?
  JUNIPER: What what?
  KEY: Your face.
  JUNIPER: No, no. Don't worry. Just getting used to them again.
  KEY: Excuse me?
  JUNIPER: I'll be fine.
  KEY: "I'll be fine"?
  JUNIPER: Here, give me the next one.
  KEY: I don't love hearing my designer using phrases like "I'll be fine".
  JUNIPER: But I will. I'm sure I will.
  KEY: We're six poems in, Em.
  JUNIPER: Oh.
  KEY: "Oh"?
  JUNIPER: No, no. It's fine. Gimme.

ROSE AND CROWN.

The girls went to the bog together.

I was jealous.

I grabbed one of the lads and asked if he fancied coming for a piss with me.

He agreed and we climbed the stairs.

I had a good old slash next to Peter.

We didn't speak but at the sink bit he asked if I was having a good night.

I said it was okay, yeah.

We went back to the group.

After a bit the girls came back.

They were laughing tons.

Also they had apparently arranged to start going to salsa lessons and they had swapped caps.

They'd had a lovely time.

I told my anecdote about the chat Peter and I had had at the sink bit.

A GORGEOUS BOY.*

I realised I was beautiful and started buying mirrors.
I would preen and pout in front of my mirrors.
I bought ninety in all and I would also talk to my mirrors.
I'd smile broadly and say, "What's up mirrors?" and, "Who here thinks I'm beautiful?"
They'd beam back at me.
My mirrors couldn't have been more on board with it all!

*JUNIPER: Ha ha.
 KEY: What?
 JUNIPER: Okay, I'm on board.
 KEY: You like this one?
 JUNIPER: I'm getting used to them again.
 KEY: Thank God for that, Em.

* KEY: Here, give me that lot. And then you take that.

JUNIPER: Someone's got a system!

KEY: "Chapter Two". And then I'll put "Chapter One" into my little red case thing.

JUNIPER: Mm.

KEY: What?

JUNIPER: Just wondering what the chapters denote.

KEY: They're just chapters, Em.

JUNIPER: Simple as that.

KEY: Well, I dunno, do I? There's twelve, Em. We can get more gin and peppermint once we've got through this one.

JUNIPER: Maybe they could be the months of the year.

KEY: Maybe. I mean they're not.

JUNIPER: Then why have 'em?

KEY: Why have chapters? You kidding me?

JUNIPER: I dunno.

KEY: The only thing I know is I'm not reading a book with no chapters. I promise I'm not, Em.

JUNIPER: You know what? I *like* the idea of January, February, *et cetera*, I must admit. In June, tons of summery poems. End with the Christmas stuff, yer know.

KEY: Well, I've gone "Chapter One", "Chapter Two". Keep it real.

JUNIPER: Just as little breakers, in between? But chapters can be so much more than that.

KEY: "Chapters can be so much more than that"? Honestly, Em, some of the things you say.

JUNIPER: You see them just as breakers, huh.

KEY: They're so people can draw breath, Em. That's what they're there for. Otherwise, it never ends.

JUNIPER: You could have October and have all your Hallowe'en ones!

KEY: I know what I *could* have, Em. I *could* have a chapter called "Gross" and have everyone squirming around in their own faeces.

JUNIPER: Never too late, that's all I'm saying.

KEY: If it was down to you, I'd have a slew of dragon ones in my St George's Day chapter.

JUNIPER: Ha ha! "Slew". Come on then, gimme.

KEY: I can't have you making smartarse comments every time I put a chapter in front of your beak, Em.

JUNIPER: No, no. I'm into it. "Chapter Two". Why not?

CHAPTER TWO.*

Chapter Two

EXCUSES, EXCUSES.*

I ate some moss and called my boss.
"Listen Ross, I've chowed down on some moss."
"I don't give a toss, you have to come in, David."

---

*JUNIPER: Ha ha, yeah bring him in.
KEY: Yeah.
JUNIPER: Cheeky sod, trying to make himself ill.
KEY: If that *is* what he's doing.
JUNIPER: Is it not?
KEY: He's just phoned his boss, that's all.
JUNIPER: His boss thinks he's trying to worm out of working though.
KEY: Yeah, yeah, looks like maybe David's tried it on before.
JUNIPER: And Ross is totally onto him.
KEY: I just think there's more going on.
JUNIPER: That's the thing with the short ones.
KEY: Yeah.
JUNIPER: There's a whole thing going on behind them.
KEY: Yeah.
JUNIPER: I love the short ones.
KEY: This is the only one this short, Em.

STRETCHING THE TAPE.

The suit guy measured me up.

He muttered the stats as he went.

I didn't exactly love the figure he was quoting for my waist.

"Pardon me?" I ejaculated.

He repeated the scandal and moved his tape to my inside leg; he was humming as he worked.

I grabbed his wrist, moved it back up onto my hip.

"Recount," I snarled.

I'm not having some bald tailor associating that kind of number with my girth.

I breathed in and told him to stretch his goddamn tape, told him we could do better.

"Thirty-eight?" he ventured.

I didn't love it, but I sensed that was as thin as he could go.

I nodded and put him back into my inner thigh.

He reported its length.

He was smiling.

There wasn't an ounce of fat on this guy.

The whole thing was rigged.

A STORM OUTSIDE.*

I was holding my pint upside down and all the beer started
pouring out.
The barman came over and pointed to the puddle of
Harvey's Sussex Best that glowed at my feet.
He whacked my Uggs with his stick and I squealed and
turned my glass back over.
I scratched his chest and begged him to shove more beer in there.
We reconvened at the bar.
As he replenished my tankard his hand wandered across the
counter and he held my wrist.
His cheeks were red and he was emitting a low growl.

* **JUNIPER:** What?
  KEY: God knows.

WOOD.

It was fucking cold and I was wearing *totally* the wrong clothes.
Just to run you through it, I'd gone for denim shorts, no
top, pop socks, sandals, my little yellow beret and a wooden
necklace.
I was freezing my nads off here!
There was nowt else for it: I *charged* into FatFace.
But my brain was frozen solid and I wasn't thinking straight
and I ended up buying sunglasses, a three-pack of scrunchies
and another wooden necklace.
I left and my torso went pale blue again as I peered back
through the window at the marvellous jumpers.
And then they disappeared as my breath lacquered the
window with a chill mist that quickly turned to frost.

TRIM.*

I went into the hairdresser's and showed him a photo of a bloke.
"I'd like a haircut like that, cheers."
He went very serious.
"That's my brother," he said.
"A little less off the fringe though," I continued, miming
scissors, licking my lips.
"Where did you get this photo of my brother?"
I rubbed my hands together and pulled out my plastic shawl.
I fixed it round my neck and did a little curtsy.
I waddled over to the chair.

---

*JUNIPER: How's he got the photo?
KEY: I dunno, Em. Ours is not to wonder why.
JUNIPER: Hang on, let me read it again.
KEY: I think up poems when I'm down the hairdresser's, Em. It's either that
    or engage with Mr Condor.
JUNIPER: Ha! I can't imagine you going to a hairdresser's.
KEY: Charming. You think I'm hacking it off with a breadknife over here?
JUNIPER: It's interesting, this one.
KEY: It's a poem, Em. Try not to talk about it as if it's a rock we've found on
    the beach.
JUNIPER: Is that what I'm doing?
KEY: Your tone. It's as if we're both wearing sarongs and examining a shell.
JUNIPER: I'm sorry, I had no idea that was how I was sounding. Let me read
    it again.
KEY: Jesus, Em. How many times you gonna read this one?
JUNIPER: Don't make them intriguing then.
KEY: With the best will in the world, I'm not going to apologise for my
    poems being intriguing.
JUNIPER: "Where did you get this photo of my brother?"
KEY: Yeah.

THE HAPPY COUPLE.

The best man didn't prepare a speech as such.
He decided he'd just see "what came to mind".
In the event, nothing really did.
He was largely silent.
Once or twice he'd look over at the bride and groom and say,
"There they are."

ACAST.*

The girl on the train asked me if she could squeeze out.
I said no because I was listening to a certain podcast.
She went quiet, looked out the window.
We went through Darlington, York.
She asked me again if she could squeeze out.
I said no again.
I said I was still listening to this same podcast.
She asked how long was left on it.
I said I didn't know.
I explained they're all different lengths because they don't
have to fit into a schedule.

---

*JUNIPER: You should do a podcast!
　KEY: I'm doing this now, Em.
　JUNIPER: You could do one with Sophie Ellis-Bextor.
　KEY: What? I don't know Sophie Ellis-Bextor.
　JUNIPER: Yet.
　KEY: Why do you want me to do a podcast with Sophie Ellis-Bextor?
　JUNIPER: I think it'd be a good fit.
　KEY: Can we focus on my anthology, do you think?
　JUNIPER: I'd listen. I'd tell my mailing list about it.
　KEY: I'm not doing a podcast with Sophie Ellis-Bextor, Em. I'm sorry.
　JUNIPER: She'll be heartbroken.
　KEY: Of course she won't, Em. She won't have known it was on the cards.

＊JUNIPER: Ooh, what did you do in Amsterdam?!
  KEY: What didn't I do in Amsterdam?
  JUNIPER: *Noooo!* Really? Drugs?
  KEY: Nope, steered clear of drugs.
  JUNIPER: Red-light district, I bet.
  KEY: Nope, steered clear of the red-light district.
  JUNIPER: Van Gogh?
  KEY: No, steered clear of the art.
  JUNIPER: Canals?
  KEY: You could hardly avoid them, Em.
  JUNIPER: You get a boat?
  KEY: No, steered clear of boats.

STAR.*

I ordered a coffee and a Kronenbourg 1664, and a damn
stingray smashed through the train window.
What the hell!!!
I asked the French guard chap if this was normal and he
indicated that we were maybe in the ocean and we'd maybe
smashed into this sea creature or something.
"But is it normal??!!!" I screamed.
The carriage was filling up with gross sea water and he said
no it wasn't normal and he was laughing nervously.
There was a small hammerhead shark nutting my boy now
and I asked Monsieur how far to Amsterdam.
He was checking his watch and bubbles were rising up from
his pantaloons.
He had an octopus round his neck.
My panini was soaked.
The girl I'd been talking to had floated up to the ceiling and
was drifting into the luggage racks.

PIGGIE.*

Someone had brought a pig to the pub.
"Here piggie, piggie!"
I was lashed, I wanted him near me.
I wanted to wrap my scarf around his
thick neck.
What I wanted more than anything else
was to create the impression that I was
with the pig

JUNIPER: Oink.
  KEY: Well, quite.

JUNIPER: Hey?

KEY: What?

JUNIPER: What have you done here?

KEY: "The Canterbury Ones".

JUNIPER: No, but as in, you've changed the title.

KEY: It's called "The Canterbury Ones".

JUNIPER: I wondered what you were doing, shuffling your papers over there.

KEY: Just leafing through my poems, that's all.

JUNIPER: Look, it's Chapter Three. But now you've called it "The Canterbury Ones".

KEY: Well, you were going on about "it's a waste", all that.

JUNIPER: You've gone mad with your Sharpie.

KEY: I've gone sane with my Sharpie, Em.

JUNIPER: So it goes "Chapter One", "Chapter Two", "The Canterbury Ones".

KEY: Apparently so.

JUNIPER: And, what? All Canterbury poems in this bit?

KEY: Ronseal, Em. Does what it says on the tin.

JUNIPER: From when you went to Canterbury.

KEY: From when I went to Canterbury. I'm actually glad it's called "The Canterbury Ones". I think it's apt.

JUNIPER: I remember talking to you when you were in Canterbury.

KEY: We had a nice chat, Em. You were walking Pongo on the beach.

JUNIPER: And all the while you were writing Canterbury poems.

KEY: Well, hang on a minute. You're talking as if I didn't watch Fargo in my Airbnb.

JUNIPER: How many Canterbury poems then?

KEY: Five, it'll be.

JUNIPER: And that's a chapter?

KEY: "The Canterbury Ones".

JUNIPER: I mean, I was all for not going "Chapter One", "Chapter Two", "Chapter Three", *et cetera* –

KEY: Careful what you wish for, Em.

JUNIPER: I know. I know that's what this is.

KEY: It's a classic Careful What You Wish For, Em.

JUNIPER: You're shuffling again.

KEY: Give the Canterbury ones a read then.

JUNIPER: While you shuffle.

KEY: While I see what's what with Chapter Four.

THE CANTERBURY
ONES.*

CANTERBURY I.*

I found myself in the ancient city of Canterbury!
Its streets were laced with cobbles and I found the terrain a bore.
I hadn't evolved the brutal hooves of the locals and lost
my footing almost immediately, crashing through the vast
window of a FatFace.
I awoke under some subtly branded sweatshirts, a bit like the
ones Grant, my friend from the clinic, might wear.
Kentish men and women were blowing air down my throat
to get me going again.
Soon my satchel was back on my shoulder and I was on my
way, clonking awkwardly up to the famous cathedral, whose
heaviest bell weighs in at almost 7,000lbs lol.

---

*JUNIPER: And here we go.
  KEY: Indeed we do.
  JUNIPER: *All* Canterbury.
  KEY: In this chapter, yeah.
  JUNIPER: Mm.
  KEY: No use saying "mm", Em. It's not going to make them be about a
     different city.
  JUNIPER: And no themes?
  KEY: Yeah, some things repeat, yeah.
  JUNIPER: Well, okay. That's something I guess.

CANTERBURY II.*

I went up Canterbury Cathedral for a giggle.
I'd been on House of Games so they gave me a good
reception and let me ring the bell.
I gave it a good old whack on the rim, and the mayor and
some of the choristers applauded.
They fed me some weird, thin Kentish mead in the courtyard
and the priest guy presented me with vouchers for FatFace.
I bought some plain swim shorts, a webbing belt and a khaki
bucket hat.
The chap on the till had heard me ringing the bell earlier
and he threw in a free strand bead bracelet and scratched my
knuckle when he handed over the bag.

---

*JUNIPER: Canterbury.
  KEY: Mm-hm.

CANTERBURY III.*

I bought an ice cream from some short-ass dweeb on the hill.
We fell out during the transaction and I ended up with the
ice cream splatted on my face, the cone springing out of my
forehead like a damn horn.
Children pointed and hollered as I clattered back through
central Canterbury.
Once I'd cooled off a little I went to White Stuff and then
into FatFace.
I won't bore you with the grizzly details of what I bought in
that shop.
It wasn't until I was posing in the changing room mirror in
my FatFace kilt that I realised there was a tiny cut just above
the circular bruise, which I had attained during the ice cream
attack I talked about in the first half of the poem.

* **JUNIPER:** Do they do kilts then?
  KEY: Dunno, guessing probably they do.
  JUNIPER: I once danced with a chap in a kilt at a wedding.
  KEY: Fuck that.
  JUNIPER: Hauled me onto the dance floor. He was spicy, this guy.
  KEY: Was he Scottish?
  JUNIPER: I dunno, didn't hear him speak.
  KEY: Don't wear one if you're not Scottish. That's my honest opinion.
  JUNIPER: I think he was Scottish, he was throwing himself into the ceilidh
       alright.
  KEY: Spin you round, did he?
  JUNIPER: His kilt was ballooning up over his mullet half the time.
  KEY: Yup. Yup. Could be Scottish.

CANTERBURY IV.

It was raining and Canterbury looked worse than ever.

I picked up some bits and pieces from M&S, as in sarnies, vegetable crisps, yum yums and a 10lb scotch egg.

I scampered into FatFace and swept a new outfit off the rails.

I threw my sodden overalls to the lad at the till and changed into my new threads.

I asked the lad if he'd like to share my grub and he said he was famished and he'd love to.

We hacked up a FatFace fleece and fashioned it into a picnic blanket.

Other people came into the shop and changed into FatFace stuff.

They'd brought food, too!

What a spread!

Outside, the grim rains savaged the city.

Inside, locals, tourists and staff chowed down on meats and pastes, rolled around amongst the pullovers, luxuriated in the vibe.

CANTERBURY V. *

I found myself in Canterbury, thank God.
I'd heard somewhere about its jams.
I ticked off that side of things in a Sainsbury's Local and
clicked open the jar on a bench not a million miles away
from FatFace.
I dunked my Barclays Premier debit card in again and again
and ultimately, when it could find no more jam, I smashed
the vessel and licked the shards clean with my tongue.
"Fan of our jams then?"
This is the lady from FatFace talking now.
She'd observed the event through the window.
"I can barely deny it."
I licked my lips and she ran two Hamble crew neck jumpers
and a straw trilby through her scanner thing.
I could hear the cathedral's bells clanging sullenly in the
middle distance and saluted hard as my garments were
bagged up.

---

*JUNIPER: And that's that. The final Canterbury poem.
   KEY: Oh God, yeah.
   JUNIPER: There's not going to suddenly be one more in the final chapter.
   KEY: No, if I had another one it would have been in this chapter.
   JUNIPER: Well.
   KEY: Well, what?
   JUNIPER: Nah, fine.
   KEY: You ever been?
   JUNIPER: Where?
   KEY: "Where?" she asks.

*JUNIPER: I mean this is insane.

KEY: What? What is?

JUNIPER: I'm really a straight-down-the-line kind of a girl, I like to think.

KEY: I don't altogether like it when you wiggle your gin and peppermint at me, Em.

JUNIPER: I'm straight-down-the-line.

KEY: You're making the ice rattle, that's what.

JUNIPER: Look at it though. You've been at it with your Sharpie again.

KEY: I don't know why we have to have a massive dust-up each time there's a new chapter.

JUNIPER: Well, what do you think? "Chapters Four – Seven". That sounds like an okay thing to you?

KEY: It's called being efficient, Em.

JUNIPER: It's called being crazy, man. You've got all the stuff there and you've just… it makes it seem like you're giving me any old thing.

KEY: Let's talk about your hair, Em. It's wild!

JUNIPER: I'd rather we had "Chapter One, Chapter Two, Chapter Three" than this.

KEY: Ha ha.

JUNIPER: What?

KEY: Someone's changed their tune.

JUNIPER: "Chapters Four – Seven". I think I'm going to throw up.

KEY: But what does it matter? Who gets excited when they see "Chapter Four" in a book? Shake it up, that's what.

JUNIPER: I'd rather see that. Then later "Chapter Seven", "Chapter Ten". I'd take that over this.

KEY: Who's getting a stiffy when they see "Chapter Ten"?

JUNIPER: What?

KEY: I just think, as long as the stuff is broken up a bit, the chapters have done their job. That's my honest opinion.

JUNIPER: So, I'm now designing a book where it says "Chapters Four – Seven" in it.

KEY: But remember how you reacted when it was all Canterbury?

JUNIPER: Can I get another gin and peppermint? This is stressing me out.

KEY: And I'll add this: when we get to the next chapter, can we not turn it into a big issue?

JUNIPER: I genuinely think you've started naming the chapters to provoke me into turning it into an issue.

KEY: Well.

JUNIPER: Look, you're already shuffling the next lot and waggling your Sharpie.

CHAPTERS
FOUR–SEVEN.*

MONDAY. *

I was feeling a little sluggish so I sacked off the day.
My boss came in.
My feet were on the desk and I was eating, to be 100% fair to myself, kebab meat and mash.
"What are you doing, pal?" my boss enquired.
"I've sacked off the day."
My boss was extremely agitated and pointed to my inbox with his thumb.
I nodded.
"Gotta say, I think that lot's starting to look a bit *tomorrowy*, dear leader."
He blew his cheeks out so far they went translucent.
I opened up my filing cabinet thing.
I pulled out a 250ml can of Pimm's and lemonade.
I tried to close my laptop with my toes.

* **JUNIPER:** Mondays.
  KEY: What?
  JUNIPER: I know what he means.
  KEY: "He"?
  JUNIPER: The chap in the poem.

A DEE IN THE LIFE.

Jack Dee
Swallowed his bee.
He came to me.
I used my brie
To lure out the bee.
I charged Jack a small fee.
£12.93.

A TIGHT SQUEEZE.*

I bought a new anorak, but it was tight as fuck.
As I forced the zip up, my body got squeezed
upwards and my head bulged and one of my
eyes popped out.
I undid my zip a little and everything
redispersed somewhat.
I stooped to pick up my eyeball.
I licked the grit off it and wedged it back in.
I blinked.
I breathed out.
The zip squeaked and crawled downwards.

---

*JUNIPER: Ha ha.
  KEY: Cheers.
  JUNIPER: You don't know why I'm laughing.
  KEY: You're laughing, Em. That's the main thing. They're supposed to be amusing.
  JUNIPER: Do you think Wordsworth –
  KEY: Let's not go down that route, Em. That kind of talk gets us nowhere.
  JUNIPER: I'm going to look up how many poems Wordsworth wrote.
  KEY: But… he and I – Wordsworth's a guy, yeah?
  JUNIPER: *William.*
  KEY: We're on different journeys. He's sat in a meadow scratching his balls trying to crank out the perfect poem, yer know.
  JUNIPER: You're writing about a tight anorak.
  KEY: We're chalk and cheese, Em.
  JUNIPER: He wrote less than four hundred, look.
  KEY: Yeah, but I don't spend days thinking, Em.
  JUNIPER: Just bang 'em out?
  KEY: They flow out quite easily my ones. I'm very lucky in that respect.

THE BLEND.

I quadruple booked myself and tried to
"blend" my appointments.
It was chaos.
It ain't easy trying to pitch your movie idea
to some big-ass Hollywood exec at the same
time as giving blood.
Meanwhile I've got my tongue in my date's
lughole and my five-a-side football team
are going ballistic, telling me to down my
Aftershock and chant stuff.
And all this on opening night of The Seagull,
the director giving me daggers every time I
miss a cue.

AH, THE DOCTOR! *

I slid into the MRI tube and the doctor
crawled in after me.
He asked me to budge up and the clonking
and sirens began.
"Why are you in here?" I enquired.
The doctor slid his glasses into his leather case
and scratched his ribs.
"I like it in here," said he, "I feel safe."
I budged up as best I could, but I could feel
his kneecap in my kidney and his tooth was
gnawing into my throat.

---

*JUNIPER: You went in the tube?
  KEY: There's no shame in it, Em.
  JUNIPER: My aunt went in the tube, she –
  KEY: Never mind your aunt, Em. I think we'll have an anecdote from me,
        won't we. Since I've *actually been in one.*
  JUNIPER: Why did you have an MRI scan anyway?
  KEY: I went in with my watch on.
  JUNIPER: No! Really? I thought they were hot on that stuff.
  KEY: The second hand burst through the screen. The nurses had to switch
        the machine off and on again.
  JUNIPER: Bet you were popular.
  KEY: Went in again, smuggled it in on my ankle.
  JUNIPER: Why'd'ya want your watch in there so much?
  KEY: I know.
  JUNIPER: But why?
  KEY: Ha ha. Sorry, I'm losing it over here!

NAUGHTY STEPS.

I woke up and my steps had gone through the roof.
I'd been out and about!
I stared at the graph.
Fuck me, I'd done 18,000 steps in my sleep.
I groped my calves.
As expected, they were piping hot and throbbing.
I scrutinised my route.
What the fuck?
I'd crossed the Thames, and *without* using one of
her famous bridges.
"You're joking me," I muttered.
I loped over to my clothes.
As suspected, they were thoroughly drenched.
Also, they weren't mine.
They were a policeman's uniform and the helmet
had a bullet hole through it.
What adventures had I had?
I reversed back into my bed, flicked on LBC.

THE LEAD.*

I got a part in a movie.
I would be the lead, yay!
I was delighted and had drinks with my wife
to celebrate my good fortune.
My part was called Superman, a flying chap
who pretended to be a journalist by day.
My wife kept on asking why he kept up his
journalism, and I kept on shoving the script
under her hooter and saying, "I don't know,
how about you read it?!"
She kept on saying, "I'm not asking to read
the script! I'm asking you to give me the most
meagre idea why you're accepting the role in
this damn picture!"

---

*JUNIPER: You got any movies coming up?
  KEY: The whole thing's skewed against the likes of me, Em.
  JUNIPER: D'oh! I like it when you crop up in things.
  KEY: A little flab around the hips and the moneymen blackball you. They
    want you nowhere near their picture.
  JUNIPER: There have been fat actors, haven't there?
  KEY: "Fat"? What???
  JUNIPER: No, just you're saying –
  KEY: Where the fuck has that come from? Fat?
  JUNIPER: No, but I'm saying, someone like John Candy –
  KEY: What the actual fuck is going on here?
  JUNIPER: I'm saying not all actors are stick thin, like a pencil.
  KEY: Candy weighed three hundred and fifty pounds, Em. Why are we
    talking about Candy?
  JUNIPER: Well, anyway, I liked you in Peep Show.
  KEY: That's not even a movie, Em. This is crazy.

CUPPA.

I opted to make a lemon and ginger tea.
It felt exotic seeing all this ginger and I
bunged in a clove of garlic too.
I also chopped a fresh red chilli in.
I had a boner now and added half a teaspoon
of sugar and grated a whole carrot into the
offending mug.
I lobbed 250g of mince in and stirred the filth
with a wooden spoon.
I presented the solution to grandma.
She pulled a face and dunked her biccie in.
I could hear it thudding against the meat and
I felt wretched.

* KEY: You're pulling that face again.

JUNIPER: That's just my face.

KEY: No chance. You've pulled that. What's up? If there's an issue then tell me.

JUNIPER: No. No issue. Just, they are, literally, *all over the place.* The poems.

KEY: But when they were all about Canterbury, you pulled it too.

JUNIPER: A decent anthology –

KEY: Which this is, Em. Which this is.

JUNIPER: What the best ones do –

KEY: I've seen anthologies, Em. I really have.

JUNIPER: Then act like it.

KEY: But I am acting like it, Em. I swear I am. Those things are chaos.

JUNIPER: I've read one that was all about autumn.

KEY: Oh, well done them. Forty poems about leaves going orange. Whoopy do.

JUNIPER: People like that. Open a glass of wine, sit in front of a roaring fire, read about the changing of the seasons.

KEY: I'd love to know how you open a glass of wine.

JUNIPER: You know what I mean.

KEY: Haven't got the first idea, Em.

JUNIPER: This one's about you getting your dolphin on –

KEY: Let me slap my poems down, Em. Let them be an anthology. Design them in such a way that they seem that way. Embrace the form, Em, for God's sake.

FLIPPER.*

I turned into a dolphin.
I rang Maud, told her the latest.
I explained I was drying out, that my flanks
were getting sore.
She said she had a girlfriend who drove a car
with a trailer on the back full of salt water.
I said, "Yeah cool, she sounds ideal."
I asked if she thought her friend would drive
to the sea with me in her trailer.
"I'm sure she would, Mike. These are the
kinds of situations she thrives on."

*JUNIPER: Ha! Is this when you came and visited me!?
   KEY: Ha, yeah! Could be!
   JUNIPER: But I'm Falmouth, not Newquay.
   KEY: Oh I sometimes change destinations. Keep my whereabouts under my hat, yer know.
   JUNIPER: Under your hat from who?
   KEY: Dunno. Just rather say Newquay. Avoid the hassle.
   JUNIPER: What hassle?
   KEY: Well, anyway, yeah that's from my trip to Falmouth.
   JUNIPER: You think you're gonna have a thousand of your Instagram followers waiting on the platform at Falmouth?
   KEY: Not if I'm putting Newquay I won't.

PRETOX.*

I bought a whole load of Pret, as in shit-tons, as in basically
a disgrace.
Almond croissants, chocolate croissants, pain aux raisins,
the mango stuff, the cheese and tomato thing, a Love
Bar, fuckloads of crisps, several Swedish meatball wraps,
chocolate mousse, people taking photos of me, me leaving
disgusted with myself.
My bag was *bulging* as I staggered across the concourse and
boarded the 9.04 to Newquay.
I was so sad looking at my bag.
I poured in my coffee and my mango smoothie and I let it
ferment, if that's the word I'm after.
I let my head fall into the bag.
I could feel my mouth opening and closing and my stomach
filling.
I could hear the train announcer talking about how we
would reach Reading soon.
He sounded appalled.
As if he was looking at me on one of his cameras.

PAPERS.

I got asked to join the army.
I didn't want to join.
I had read an article about a soldier who
hadn't enjoyed it.
I emailed the lady back explaining this.
She sent me three more articles with soldiers
testifying that it was fun.
I read the articles and reread them.
God, it sounded good.
I emailed Trish again.
"Okay, I'm in," I said, "Let's do this, Trish."

NUISANCE.*

I sat down with a couple in the boozer.
Didn't even ask, just pulled a stool over, slammed my pint
down, said "cooee" or similar.
Ha ha!
The fella's chat was shit, I must say.
I started snorting my derision and that buggered up his flow
even more.
I kept mimicking his divvy accent and passing notes to the
girl asking her what she was doing with this clown.
They moved to a different table.
I got myself another drinkie, went and joined them.
I was being a real pain in the neck!
Blighting their evening!

---

*KEY: Do us a favour will you, Em?
JUNIPER: Go on.
KEY: Can you design the pub ones up a bit, eh?
JUNIPER: Oh right, as in beer all over the place type of thing.
KEY: Or just a magic "P" for "pub" kinda thing?
JUNIPER: And then sandwiches everywhere for the ones set in Pret, ha ha!
KEY: No, Em just the pub ones for now. There's just lots of them, is all. It'll
make 'em think I'm doing it deliberately.
JUNIPER: Do a pub chapter?
KEY: Yeah, well. I'm thinking we do it this-a-way.
JUNIPER: Do you want me to make it look like the poems are in
pint glasses, and we're looking through the glass at them?
KEY: Em, I honestly don't know what you're talking about.

FIGHT.*

"I want to be with you."
"No."
A pause.
"Come on, Flo."
"It's too late."
A pause.
"Why?"
"Don't do this, Shay."
"Do what? Fight?"
A pause.
"I'm trying to fight for you, Flo."
"I know you are, Shay, and I'm
telling you to stop doing it and
eat your pie."

---

*JUNIPER: This one's more… a dialogue.
  KEY: Yuh.
  JUNIPER: Funny.
  KEY: Cheers.
  JUNIPER: No, it's funny having a dialogue. And then telling us it's a poem.
  KEY: Who the fuck is "us"?
  JUNIPER: The audience then.
  KEY: You're not the audience, Em.
  JUNIPER: No?
  KEY: No. It works best when you detach yourself from the material.
  JUNIPER: I like the material.
  KEY: You're with me, Em.
  JUNIPER: Oh, okay.
  KEY: Against *them*.
  JUNIPER: Against?
  KEY: No, not against. But… you know what I mean. You're over here.
  JUNIPER: With you.
  KEY: That's when it works best, Em.

SPECIALIST.

I went to a "specialist bar".
I ordered a beer and someone came over with a
zebra and asked if I wanted to fuck him.
I fucked the zebra and sat on a table in a corner,
waited for my Amstel.
A man came over, put my pint down in front of me.
He went away and then came back with
complimentary Twiglets.
"Excuse me," I grabbed his cuff, "Says outside it's a
specialist bar. Just wondering, specialist how?"
He smiled and wandered away.
After some time, he came back with a "menu" of
board games.

⁕JUNIPER: What's happened here?

KEY: Halfway.

JUNIPER: But it's not halfway. Look at all that crap you've got there.

KEY: Okay, but it is halfway. As in… I mean…

JUNIPER: It's literally not. I'm looking at all the stuff we've read and all this stuff we've still got to read. It's just not halfway. It's literally not.

KEY: Well, no, I know "literally" it's not.

JUNIPER: Then don't put "halfway" and make me design a page with it.

KEY: I'm just saying psychologically it's nice for people to know they've broken the back of it.

JUNIPER: But you're telling them they're further in than they are.

KEY: Em, if I tell these people they've only done a third it'll be demoralising. Trust me.

JUNIPER: Look at all the bundles, this is chaos.

KEY: "Hello reader, you've got fucking tons of this left."

JUNIPER: I'm saying don't say anything.

KEY: Nah, nice to have a pick-me-up.

JUNIPER: This is gonna bugger my contents page *right up*.

KEY: Yeah, it'll look funny, I'll give you that.

JUNIPER: It's like when you tell me you're five minutes away and you've not even left your house.

KEY: Ha ha.

JUNIPER: What?

KEY: Yeah, it is like that.

JUNIPER: Well, I don't know why you're smirking. That's not a good thing.

KEY: You honestly expect me to use phrases like "I'm forty minutes away minimum". You'd lose your shit, Em.

JUNIPER: I'd rather that than sit with my coffee getting cold looking at my bleedin' watch.

KEY: You can get them to top it up with hot water, that's what I do.

JUNIPER: Well.

KEY: Oh, don't say "well" like that.

JUNIPER: Can we take a break?

KEY: Um… I mean, yeah.

JUNIPER: Go and have a look at the church, have an ice cream.

KEY: Yeah, go on then. A halfway Magnum.

JUNIPER: It's not halfway.

KEY: Great, we can have another Magnum at actual halfway then.

JUNIPER: Ask that old clown to guard your poems, will ya?

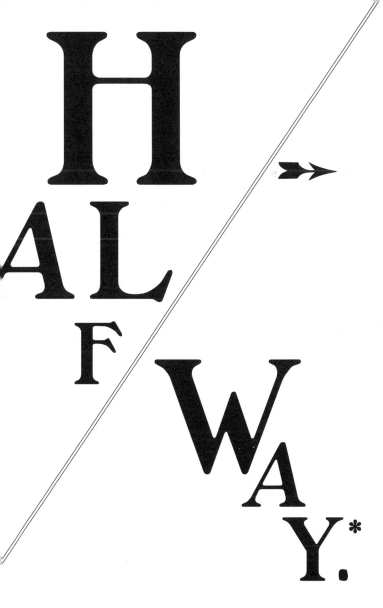

JUNIPER: This is obviously a goad. You're goading me.

KEY: I enjoyed our walk, I must say.

JUNIPER: "Hairdressing, London, Ambition, and The News". Really?

KEY: It's what's in the chapter. A poem about hairdressing, some about London –

JUNIPER: How can you even do poems about "the news"?

KEY: *That's* your question?

JUNIPER: It is a bit, yeah. Because look –

KEY: I've got a poem about everyone striking, look. I've got one about the Tories.

JUNIPER: Conservatives.

KEY: That's the idea.

JUNIPER: I never thought I'd say it, but I'd take more poems about people turning into dolphins at this stage.

KEY: I think I'd rather you keep your hooter out of which actual poems I choose, Em.

JUNIPER: I don't know why. You're always welcome to give me constructive feedback on the design side.

KEY: I know, and yet I don't. I let you get on with it.

JUNIPER: I'm trying to. I just prefer the little ones, where someone has some problems, that's all.

KEY: I hate us two falling out, Em.

JUNIPER: We're not falling out.

KEY: Then stop hitting the table. That man's looking at us.

JUNIPER: But it's… news is… news. So you can't print it a year after the event.

KEY: People have been writing poems about world events for years, Em. Do you know what I like?

JUNIPER: Don't try and change the subject. You can't have a book printed in 2023 that –

KEY: Do you know what *I* like?

JUNIPER: You're just trying to change the subject.

KEY: I'm not.

JUNIPER: What do you like then?

KEY: When people use one of those blowtorch things to brown meringues.

JUNIPER: Okay.

KEY: Okay?

JUNIPER: I mean, that's got nothing to do with anything, but –

KEY: Well, it's something I like, anyway.

JUNIPER: Okay, let's go through the poems, then.

HAIRDRESSING, LONDON, AMBITION, AND THE NEWS.*

＊JUNIPER: You wrote this in Falmouth!

KEY: Someone's perked up.

JUNIPER: I liked it when you came to Falmouth.

KEY: It's nice there, Em. You've got a good thing going down there, that's for sure.

JUNIPER: We're not usually that drunk, I promise!

KEY: You were great hosts.

JUNIPER: That happens about once a year.

KEY: The ocean?

JUNIPER: It's just we were lashed and Blummel can get a bit of a bee in her bonnet when she's had a few Strongbows and the next thing you know —

KEY: Sploosh!

JUNIPER: The 3am dunk.

KEY: Blummel's wild.

JUNIPER: She's talking about getting a campervan thing, driving round America.

KEY: It was a memorable night, Em.

QUENCHED.*

My pal offered to buy me a drink and, almost simultaneously, so did another pal.

I said yes to both – fuck it – even though I knew I already had *another one* on the way.

The three chumps returned with my beers and, you've guessed it, it all kicked off.

I held my own as best I could and, in the midst of this grubby hullabaloo, even raised my thumb to my hairdresser, who, encouragingly, was now also at the bar.

I mimed for him to bring me an ice bucket, too.

The plan being, I'd pour my freebies into the bucket, and guzzle from it like a mad Dalmatian.

See how they liked that.

ACTION!

Celebs went on strike!

A mass walkout; carnage.

It was all to do with getting the fees up for things like opera singing, appearing on House of Games, cooking pies on telly, *et cetera*.

All the stars laid down their tools.

Gower, Sugar, Balding, the lot.

The government went into panic mode, brought in everyday Joes to pick up the slack.

But these guys got eviscerated, the public weren't having 'em.

They didn't want these pointless cunts hosting Bargain Hunt and clattering around on Strictly.

They took to the streets demanding their celebs back, waggling placards.

"Pay 'em what they want!"

"Bring back Mangan!"

The world was a grey place without the actual Graham Norton sat on his bleeding hot seat, interviewing Sheridan Smith about her latest ITV thing.

YOUNG LOVERS.

I sat near a couple down the boozer.
Young lovers lol.
They were all over each other, these two, I'll give 'em that.
I angled myself away, considered the rim of my tankard.
These two didn't seem too fussed about privacy, but I gave them what I could.
They started "going through the gears" and it got a bit more appalling.
His hands were all over her forearms and he kept on saying "koochi koochi coo", all that mush.
I asked them politely to get a room and that seemed to fuel their desires, if anything.
The next thing I knew they were – horrible phrase – fucking on the pool table.
This was all I needed.
I shoved a couple of fifty p's in the slots and *released the balls.*
I hurled them at this thick gentleman's ass.
Really pelted this guy.
I wanted to bump some decorum into this primitive dog.

＊JUNIPER: Basically, anyone with half a brain and a laptop could be
  Chancellor. I heard about this.
KEY: Yeah, you would have done, Em.
JUNIPER: It was on the BBC News website.
KEY: It would have been, for sure.
JUNIPER: Who's Eddie Howe then?
KEY: Newcastle manager.
JUNIPER: Oh right. As in an unlikely bloke to be Chancellor, that's the gag.
KEY: I think he could have done a job, if I'm honest, Em.
JUNIPER: Really?
KEY: Sorted Newcastle out, didn't he?

THE ONLY MAN FOR THE JOB.*

There was nothing else for it.
Eddie Howe was appointed as chancellor.
"Well, if I do it, I do it my way, Liz."
"Just fucking do it, can you, Ed, sort out the mess, man."
"Email me the numbers then, doll, I'm in."
Eddie emerged from No. 11.
He had the letters EH on his training top and he chewed
gum as he approached the mic.
He looked *fresh*.
No red suitcase bollocks for the big man; he unzipped his
Adidas kitbag, whipped out some notes and an abacus,
clutched the lectern.
He smiled and the debt seemed to melt away.
"It's okay," his voice was like warm toffee, "Ed's here now."
The markets stabilised as the saviour mixed his pragmatic
fiscal stuff in with some half-decent anecdotes about Jonjo
Shelvey and the Saudis.

✱ JUNIPER: Ha ha. Did this happen?
KEY: I'm a poet, Em. I deal in make-believe.
JUNIPER: It has the ring of truth.
KEY: That's my skill.
JUNIPER: I can imagine them leering at you, trying to work it out.
KEY: They were lashed, Em. I was trying to write.
JUNIPER: Write what?
KEY: The poem.
JUNIPER: This one?
KEY: I go up the pub, I have a scribble.
JUNIPER: How were you trying to write this poem before they'd come over though?
KEY: Huh?
JUNIPER: How were you already writing this poem before the action in it had happened in real life?
KEY: Life imitating art, I guess.
JUNIPER: Oh, okay. I guess.

DO I KNOW YOU FROM SOMEWHERE?*

Some chaps were looking at me down the boozer.
They were googling me, too.
I marched over to them.
"You got a question, ask *me*."
I was snarling so hard my lips were bruising.
"We recognise you but we don't know what from."
"Cry me a river."
I dunked my snout into my pint, I wanted it to end.
"What shows you in then?" the chap on the cider asked.
I reluctantly listed one or two of the classics.
He nodded but it wasn't exactly penny-drop territory.
One of them suggested I was potentially from The Brittas
Empire.
I said what the hell and asked him how old he thought I was.
He started googling again, and I snapped.
"I thought we weren't googling?!"
I plunged his iPhone into his Boddingtons and kept it in
there 'til it had stopped bubbling.

THE DARK WEB.*

I went on the dreaded dark web.
It was very interesting out there.
I found a "dark shop" and ordered sweetcorn.
They were very polite but there was something
bleak in the air.
Staff were wearing leather masks and when my
sweetcorn arrived and I opened the tin up, I
discovered a penis in there.
I was, to say the least, interested to know whose
penis this was.
I logged back into the dark web and trudged back
up to the shop.
It was full of bees now, unfortunately, and a far-
right guy was flying a drone in the freezer section.

---

*JUNIPER: What is "the dark web"?
 KEY: Dunno.
 JUNIPER: Oh, okay.
 KEY: Horrid, probably.
 JUNIPER: Did you research it?
 KEY: Naw. I'm having nothing to do with it.
 JUNIPER: So how did you write the poem?
 KEY: Same as always.
 JUNIPER: Bang anything down, type of thing?
 KEY: I'm sure the shops on the dark web are nasty old places, Em.
 JUNIPER: Yeah.
 KEY: I'm sure I won't get complaints from the dark web saying I've stitched
   them up.

A BEAUTIFUL FRINGE.

The hairdresser showed me the back of my
head with her mirror.
I was surprised to see she had bored a hole into
my skull and installed a shrewlike creature.
I frowned.
"Thank you."
I paid up and walked up the hill.
I could feel this damn shrew thing scratching
about behind my eyes.
I didn't half love my fringe though.

JUNIPER: You ever gonna take *me* to the snooker?

KEY: Erm.

JUNIPER: It's played on baize.

KEY: No, I know, Em. That's what you always say. To try and show you know what you're talking about.

JUNIPER: Ken Doherty.

KEY: Is a player, yes.

JUNIPER: The triangle.

KEY: Yes, that's what they use to put the reds into their formation.

JUNIPER: I'd get on fine at the snooker.

SNOOKER LOOPY.*

I opted to climb up a gantry, put the brakes on the traffic for a while.
I D-locked myself to some mad rivet and unfurled my banner.
Bugger me! I'd brought the wrong one.
I'd only gone and packed my bloody "I ♥ Judd Trump" one from the snooker!
This was all I needed.
Well, anyway, it was the only banner I had, so I stretched it out and awaited developments.
The honking and fist waggling was in full flow now and I dropped my D-lock key with the stress of it all.
I imagined the press trying to reach out to Judd for a comment and I felt awful, frankly.
This had *nothing* to do with him.
I peered through my binoculars.
A chap in stonewashed jeans had climbed the next gantry.
He had a Judd banner too.
For fuck's sake!
We'd got momentum.

* JUNIPER: Oh gawd. *That* summer.
KEY: Finally! Not sticking the boot in about one of my chapter titles.
JUNIPER: It was a scorcher, eh?
KEY: I just submitted to it, Em. It was absolutely dominant.
JUNIPER: Too hot for Emily Juniper, put it that way.
KEY: Let's make no bones about it, Em. It was a record-breaker.
JUNIPER: Like Erling Haaland.
KEY: What do you know about Erling Haaland?
JUNIPER: I know he loves to net.
KEY: He tore up the record books is what he did, Em.
JUNIPER: How do you defend against that? He's a monster, plain and simple.
KEY: I expect his parents would argue otherwise.
JUNIPER: Happy to have it out with them. Have they seen him play?
KEY: Am I ordering more booze, do we think?
JUNIPER: I just don't know how you wrote them, in that heat.
KEY: I found refuge in the cellar. I wrote amongst the wines.
JUNIPER: Hottest summer since –
KEY: 1976, Em. Spent the whole thing in my mother's belly.
JUNIPER: The '76 one?
KEY: Of course, Em. No way she's doing that in 2022.
JUNIPER: You're too big for a start-off.
KEY: And she's 78. No, those days are behind us, thank God.
JUNIPER: I hate the heat, me.
KEY: Codswallop. You love it, Em.
JUNIPER: I'm going red just thinking about it.
KEY: You are. Look, the backs of your hands have puffed up.
JUNIPER: Emily Juniper's not built for those temperatures.
KEY: I always had you down as a sun-rat, Em.
JUNIPER: Within reason.
KEY: You get to wear your wide-brimmers!
JUNIPER: Emily Juniper doesn't need it to be summer to wear her
   wide-brimmers.
KEY: Good point.
JUNIPER: Emily Juniper will wear her wide-brimmers to a panto, don't worry
   about that side of things.
KEY: And pity the poor sod sat behind her.
JUNIPER: I take it off when the panto starts, thank you.
KEY: Oh, okay.
JUNIPER: Buttons comes on, the wide-brimmer comes off, I promise you that.

IN THE SUMMERTIME.*

CLACKER.

It was *so* sunny!
When Ray Wells staggered back inside he was
as red as a lobster.
Also, he had developed pincers.
His wife reeled backwards on seeing this
abomination.
She screamed as he clacked and mewed.
She spat at him and started bringing up other
instances where he had in some way let her
down or been an arsehole.

A DAY AT THE CRICKET.

I went up the cricket.
It was in Nottingham this week and the game was shivering
on your friend and mine: the knife edge.
Oh boy, did I want to get involved!
Fortunately, one of the stewards recognised me from House
of Games and said he'd see what he could do.
He used his walkie-talkie thing for a bit and eventually
smiled at yours truly.
It was decided I'd go in after Ben Foakes and pretty soon I
found myself batting with the great Joe Root himself.
Boy, did those Kiwis bowl fast!
The gleaming cherry whizzed by my ears and the crowd bayed.
Eventually I got the hang of it and by the end of my innings
I found I had a bit more time and even played a couple of
cover drives that pierced the field and the boozy orks in the
Radcliffe Road End brayed and hooted.
I got too cute of course, got out trying to switch hit Boult,
and I said my goodbyes to the great Rooty.
He thanked me for helping out and asked if I'd been in
Ghosts and I wandered back up to my seat, peeling off my
pads as I went.
The steward from before crouched at my feet.
He congratulated me on my run-a-ball sixty-five and handed
back my pint.
He lingered a moment longer and I ruffled his white hair
with my batting glove.

THE HEAT.*

It was hot as hell and my neck melted into my collar.

I purchased ice cream and had my secretary slather it on as a salve.

Sweat trickled down his wrist as he worked in the raspberry ripple and cone.

We bemoaned the sun and its sickening conduct and encased ourselves in puffer jackets in protest.

We stood in the shadow of the ice cream van and willed the vendor to push his produce into our mouths.

He attached a hose to his nozzle and the generator whirred as our stomachs filled and our temperatures dropped like stones.

We climbed under the vehicle and held one another.

It was cool down there.

Woodlice and earthworms crawled amongst us.

My secretary pressed them against his forehead.

Respite.

---

*JUNIPER: This is what I'm talking about.

  KEY: Bugger me, it was hot, Em.

  JUNIPER: We went swimming down in the harbour.

  KEY: Well, you must live your life, Em. I've always said that.

  JUNIPER: The fishermen had stripped off.

  KEY: The sun was beating hard, Em. There were weather warnings.

  JUNIPER: They just dived in. They were crimson these fellas, they were wailing.

  KEY: Not the day to be crouching in a Mackintosh.

  JUNIPER: They weren't crouching in anything. I saw about thirty cocks that afternoon.

  KEY: Excuse me?

  JUNIPER: The fish and chip shop melted and slid into the sea.

9.45 (DOORS AT 9.30).*

The Queen announced a short run at the Soho Theatre.
She felt it was *Her moment*, so fuck it, book the place, see who
salutes.

It would be anecdotes really, a conversational hour, going
on about countries she'd been to, various dalliances she'd
had and piss-ups she'd attended in Her twenties and thirties,
plus a couple of costume changes and a big song-and-dance
number to finish.

The run sold out almost immediately (and bear in mind, this
was in the main space) and she announced a third week.

Of course, she knew the critics would be sharpening their
knives, calling Her a relic and the rest of it.

But she couldn't give a fuck about that anymore.

---

*JUNIPER: Poor old bird. Doesn't seem like five minutes since we were
waggling our flags for Her.
KEY: She was something else, that woman.
JUNIPER: I bought an apron with Her body on it.
KEY: Aye. They broke the mould when they made Her.
JUNIPER: I had to go to a street party, too.
KEY: "Had to"?
JUNIPER: Well, I showed my face anyhow.
KEY: I bloody loved my one. They had a ceilidh band and there were scones
someone had clearly made.
JUNIPER: Oh.
KEY: And then lots of kegs of beer someone had organised. And I met a girl
called Plum.
JUNIPER: Ha ha!
KEY: It was a day to rejoice, Em. Plain and simple.
JUNIPER: Poor old Queenie.
KEY: I know. I know. 'Twas no sort of age, Em.

THE VICINITY.*

My friend reached out.

It transpired we were both in Cornwall.

He started saying it was "a sign" and that we should meet up.

I said I didn't want any hassle when I was down there.

He asked how meeting up was "a hassle"?

He was raising his voice.

I could hear the veins on his neck popping out beyond his shoulders.

Why did I wanna travel ninety minutes cross-county on some weird local bus to spend an hour in a fucked-up pub with this animal?

"I'm here to write, Biffy," I lied.

I could hear him pulling his fridge over and stamping on it.

I could hear his mother trying to calm him and get the fridge back on its feet.

I could hear the waves and the gulls beyond.

---

*JUNIPER: Poor old Biffy.
  KEY: I know.
  JUNIPER: You met up with *me* though.
  KEY: I did. I always will, Em.
  JUNIPER: So I'm not Biffy.
  KEY: No, Em.
  JUNIPER: So who actually is Biffy?
  KEY: Biffy's his real name, Em. That's a big part of the problem, I think. Biffy's Biffy.
  JUNIPER: Christ.

SO SUNNY.*

Sunny trudged across the yard.
His bandana hardened under the sun.
As he walked, so his skin calcified.
He slowed to a stop and his flesh darkened as
the sun dried him like a nut.
He stood, stock still under the basketball hoop.
Then he teetered.
And fell.
And shattered into a thousand pieces on the
concrete.

---

*JUNIPER: One of the fishermen's feet ignited.
  KEY: Pardon me?
  JUNIPER: Just too hot.
  KEY: How do you mean ignited?
  JUNIPER: You know the bit I like? When it cools down a bit at around 8pm.
      Fix myself a gin and peppermint, drape myself over my trellis. Bliss.
  KEY: The fisherman, Em. What are you talking about? His feet caught fire,
      are we saying?
  JUNIPER: Pat Cloud.

KEY: And his feet caught fire?

JUNIPER: His left foot. He'd lost his sandal.

KEY: Out at sea?

JUNIPER: God, no. Pat can't swim, this was at the harbour. The sun was bouncing off the maritime museum. His foot started smoking and then –

KEY: Okay, Em. I get the picture.

JUNIPER: Had to hot-foot it to the hospital.

KEY: Ha ha.

JUNIPER: It's not funny. They couldn't extinguish it, sent him back down to the ocean, told him not to come back 'til it was "completely out".

KEY: The hospital sent the fisherman back to the ocean?

JUNIPER: Pat Cloud.

KEY: Yes, I get that he's called Pat Cloud.

JUNIPER: They wouldn't dress it 'til it had stopped glowing, basically.

KEY: What were the other fishermen doing?

JUNIPER: Sheltering from the sun. They'd seen what happened to Pat.

KEY: Did they save his foot?

JUNIPER: Yes.

KEY: Thank God.

JUNIPER: I mean, as in he's had it mounted. Like in a glass box thing. It's all charred and they've put moss around it.

KEY: Moss?

JUNIPER: The green furry thing.

KEY: No, I know what moss is, Em.

JUNIPER: I bet his charred foot looks lush on the moss.

KEY: You haven't seen it?

JUNIPER: He's ever so cheerful, considering what he's been through.

KEY: So he's… what's he got instead of a foot then?

JUNIPER: What do you mean "instead of a foot"?

KEY: I mean… I don't know what I mean.

JUNIPER: He hasn't put something different on there.

KEY: Has he not got a plastic foot.

JUNIPER: I don't know.

KEY: You don't know?

JUNIPER: He wears his long boots.

KEY: Ah.

JUNIPER: So I haven't seen whatever he's got there now.

KEY: Ah. Okay.

JUNIPER: I couldn't believe it when he told me all about it.

KEY: No. It's a mad story.

JUNIPER: It's worse if you know Pat.

KEY: You've not seen his new foot or the mounted burnt one?

JUNIPER: He's the nicest guy, Pat is.

* KEY: Em?

JUNIPER: Whatever, just give me the poems. The chapters are your business. Get me another gin and peppermint. Get me fags.

KEY: Please'd be nice. Oh.

JUNIPER: What?

KEY: That look again.

JUNIPER: Yes, that look again.

KEY: I'll get you another gin and peppermint. *Sir!*

JUNIPER: Tim! Don't click your fingers at him! Please!

AMSTERDAM
AND DATING.*

CROSSOVER.*

I went on a date and tried to look for "common ground".
We had both met (different) people called Keith Hughes.
We had both been to restaurants in the late '90s (though her experience had been very different).
One of us had been to Silverstone, and we both liked people-watching.
We stopped talking and watched the people for a bit.
She loved it.
She was clapping like a seal at a man trying to put his coat on.
She was losing her shit, pissing herself at this poor cunt.
Firing beer mats at him.
Shouting abuse.

JUNIPER: This a real date?
KEY: Does it look real?
JUNIPER: Ha ha. I can imagine you on dates.
KEY: No, you can't.
JUNIPER: Sat there with your little notepad.
KEY: No.
JUNIPER: Scribbling away when she pops to the bathroom.
KEY: This is a scandal.
JUNIPER: Chucking your book in your satchel as she floats back in.
KEY: "Satchel"? You're joking, aren't you.
JUNIPER: "Was I long? Did you miss me?"
KEY: "Nah, I was writing a poem."
JUNIPER: Ha ha! See! I can so imagine it. I can so see it in my own mind!

MY ORANGE LIFE I.*

I found myself in Amsterdam of all places.

I quickly got stoned off my tits and scuttled into your friend and mine, the red-light district.

That place, *honestly*.

I kept on banging on all the windows telling anyone who'd listen I was in love with them.

Ultimately one of the entrepreneurs asked me to put my money where my mouth was and I retreated to a gallery to lick my wounds/appreciate Rembrandt's latest offerings.

I almost felt ill sat before the big man's pictures.

I tugged on my latest dooby and squinted at the sheer competence at play here.

I was in a blissful state and my mind turned to thoughts of what paint *actually* was.

Who exactly dreamed up making thick colourful liquids and splurting it onto canvas?

Why the hell was red red?

---

*JUNIPER: The famous Amsterdam trip.
  KEY: Yuh.
  JUNIPER: Stoned off your tits.
  KEY: Chap in the poem is.
  JUNIPER: And you?
  KEY: I already said. Not a single plume of Dutch smoke entered these lungs
     of mine, Em. No lights of red hue troubled these irises of mine.
  JUNIPER: And no boats? That's still your story?
  KEY: Zero, Em. That stuff doesn't interest me.

HOOKED.*

I caught my eye on a hook on the way to my date.

I spoke to the *maître d'*.

"Bit of a situation, pal."

I opened my palm, showed him my rancido eye.

"Oh." His face was white, like a bedsheet.

I gestured to my socket.

"Gonna need a patch, old bean."

I pointed at the beautiful girl next to the waterwheel.

The *maître d'* recovered his composure and now his face was more or less bellowing the phrase "I see".

He reached under his desk and handed me a bright red surgical eyepatch.

"How did you do it?" he enquired, as he pinged the elastic against the back of my neck and straightened my tie.

"Hook." I said, setting off towards Angela.

---

*JUNIPER: You love a waterwheel, don't ya?
  KEY: I've just always had a nice time when I've been in the vicinity.
  JUNIPER: Are you having a nice time now?
  KEY: With that great thing swishing round?
  JUNIPER: My dad used to say that they were what powered the rivers.
  KEY: Jesus wept.
  JUNIPER: Quite sweet.
  KEY: And you believed that shit?
  JUNIPER: I was five.
  KEY: Obviously it's the flow of the river that turns the wheel.
  JUNIPER: I know, it's like saying that windmills make it windy.
  KEY: Another one of his?
  JUNIPER: But he's saying it for a laugh.
  KEY: I should hope so, Em. That stuff's fucking crazy.

MY ORANGE LIFE II.

I noticed I was still in Amsterdam.
I incinerated a spliff and breathed it up.
The hit I got sat there in that caff, fuck me.
The next thing I knew I was in the Dutch version of FatFace
and the garments were *alive*.
It was interesting being amongst the hoodies and granddad
shirts in an altered state.
I felt like I was in an enchanted forest, if you must know.
I began trying on different combinations of their wonderful togs.
I wasn't in my right mind and was playing, shall we say, *fast and
loose* with the colours and styles.
The proprietor nibbled a brownie and purred.
Sometimes he'd vaguely point me in the direction of some
flip-flops or a wooden necklace that he thought might
"complete" one of my mad outfits.

FEEDBACK.*

My date asked me to sound a little bit
brighter, more positive.
I took her note on board, tried again.
She said I was certainly getting closer to the
tone she was after but asked if I could maybe
push it even further.
"You look wonderful!" I cooed.
She stared at me across our pies.
"Much more like it," she said, her voice
warm, engaging, syrupy.

---

*JUNIPER: Should I buy a chapel, do you think?
  KEY: In what sense?
  JUNIPER: What "what sense"? Just buy a chapel.
  KEY: Why would you buy a chapel?
  JUNIPER: I know, right.
  KEY: Can we just go through the poems? Focus, Em.
  JUNIPER: I am. Is this one set in your local?
  KEY: Now I'm thinking about this chapel. What's the chapel, Em?
  JUNIPER: No, you're a hundred per cent right. It's madness
     buying a chapel. Ignore me.
  KEY: Where is it, Em? You gonna be a priest? What's
     happening, Em?
  JUNIPER: No, let's do this. "Syrupy". Can a voice be syrupy,
     do we think?

·89·

DEAR ALL.

Oh gawd.

A worst-case scenario.

I had *thought* I'd texted Dolly B, inviting her to join me for a romantic dins in the new French restaurant next to the printing shop.

But of course, you've guessed it, I'd accidentally texted *everyone in my phone.*

At the appointed hour I had about two hundred and fifty contacts swirling around my candle-riddled table.

I won't bore you with the grizzly details.

But the names Uncle Rodney, Stephen Merchant, Emma costume Drunk Histories, Rob opera singer, and Billie PBJ should give you a flavour of the surplus.

The proprietor was yelling at me and, to be fair, I was yelling at my grizzly throng.

I was barking, "Dolly B, Dolly B!"

As if I was on some noisy battlefield, hunting down my favourite soldier.

I was shovelling these other nobodies out the way.

I wanted them out.

I wanted my princess sat down on her rightful chaise.

Get some broiled pig's feet into her cakehole.

A THORNY SITUATION.*

I sat with my single red rose.
My date had unfortunately stood me up and now I was
staring down the barrel of sleeping with this damn rose.
I poured a gin and tonic over it, crumbled some beef Hula
Hoops onto its petals.
The bar staff were all gawping at me, of course.
Making smart-arse comments, too.
I exited stage left.
"Come on, Beryl!" I asserted, "We're out of here."
And now the bar staff started using *that* as ammo.
Having a go at me for naming my flower.
Making all sorts of comments about Beryl being an old-
fashioned name.
The works, basically.
Beryl's thorns cajoled my palm as we blew into the street.
She suggested we go for food.

---

*JUNIPER: Ha ha. You ever been stood up?
  KEY: Behave.
  JUNIPER: Am I taking that as a yes?
  KEY: Of course you're taking it as a bleeding yes, Em.
  JUNIPER: Ha ha.
  KEY: Well, have you?
  JUNIPER: I can imagine you sitting there with your little dating shirt on,
      fiddling with the beer mats –
  KEY: "Dating shirt"? What the…???

MY ORANGE LIFE III.

I decided I'd have one last poke around the
Rijksmuseum.
I was buggered if I was boarding my train without
getting an eyeful of Vermeer first.
I was quietly purring in front of Willem Drost's
Cimon and Pero when an old-school jobsworth laid
a palm on my shoulder.
He told me I had to put my stuff in the cloakroom,
way down on floor zero, by the way.
I'd learnt a smattering of Dutch and invited him to
go fuck himself.
His English was firing on all cylinders, of course.
He called me a moron and said I looked like I was in
a departure lounge.
He waggled his thumbs at my 65l Karrimor rucksack
and my House of Games carry-on suitcase.
There was nothing else for it.
I pointed at the canvas.
The soppy old sod became very emotional.
As he lost himself in the tragic oils, I took the
opportunity to gather my personal effects and
scamper to the museum café, where, let's be fair,
I ate a pizza, two mousses and a large glass of
champagne.

IN LOVE.*

An in-love boy went round the girl's house.
He flung rocks at her window.
After what seemed like an eternity, she appeared at
the window.
She leaned out and a rock glanced off her teeth.
The in-love boy stared up at this beautiful creature,
his eyes as wide as trays.
She blinked down at him, her Popeye t-shirt loose
and sleepy.
"I am in love," the in-love boy said.
She nodded down at him.
He threw one more rock.
"Hold on, Dan – I'll come and let you in."

---

*JUNIPER: Sweet.
KEY: Mm-hm.

JUNIPER: Oh, so *now* we're going down the month route?

KEY: You were past caring five seconds ago.

JUNIPER: I think months is the way to do it. I said that!

KEY: Well, there you go then. Here's a month: September.

JUNIPER: Well, yeah. But only if that's what we're doing. I mean you're changing the chapters as we go along and that worries me. As long as you organise them all so that they make sense once we're done here.

KEY: Well, I was happy with it being "Chapter One", "Chapter Two" *et cetera*.

JUNIPER: I don't mind that either, if that's what you want to do.

KEY: That was what I *wanted* to do, Em. That was how they were in my little case when I marched in here.

JUNIPER: Well, I think we should have stuck with that.

KEY: But it was you who started having a pop at them, Em! Sorry for raising my voice, but that's what started me off. I feel like I'm chasing my tail over here.

JUNIPER: It's chaos.

KEY: It's a mess, Em. We're saying the same thing.

JUNIPER: All this scribbling and your little face when you hand them to me.

KEY: What little face?

JUNIPER: Come here, don't get yourself in a state.

KEY: You're very good with me, Em. Very patient. You never really get the credit for that side of things.

JUNIPER: It's just… I don't want it to be called "September" if it's just stuff that doesn't have any relevance to anything or you've stuffed a bunch of Christmas in there.

KEY: "A bunch of Christmas". I've done no such thing.

JUNIPER: Well, go on, let's see them then.

KEY: It's got one about my birthday in it.

JUNIPER: Great.

KEY: My birthday's in September.

JUNIPER: I know. Let's have a look then.

KEY: I share it with Sir Keir Starmer.

JUNIPER: So you keep telling me.

KEY: And Keanu Reeves. So make of that what you will.

JUNIPER: The three musketeers.

KEY: Well, anyway. I'm just saying.

JUNIPER: Do you ever get told you look like Sir Keir?

KEY: Excuse me?

JUNIPER: Come on. Gimme September.

SEPTEMBER.*

*JUNIPER: Couldn't you just wait *one chapter?* Jesus!

KEY: What?

JUNIPER: Well this! Put it in October.

KEY: But the next chapter *isn't* October.

JUNIPER: This is blatantly Hallowe'eny, and yet it's stuffed in September and it makes me so mad.

KEY: It's based on a true –

JUNIPER: What do you mean the next chapter isn't October? You're crazy. I'm making it October, when I design it.

KEY: Then we're done.

JUNIPER: I promise, I'm calling it October. I'm shoving this one in it, I'm writing other poems. All about Hallowe'en. This is killing me.

KEY: It's Chapter Ten, Em.

JUNIPER: Aaaaaaaaaghhhhh!!!

KEY: It doesn't mean anything, Em.

JUNIPER: Hmmmpf.

KEY: Em, your bottom lip's gone up over your nose.

JUNIPER: Because I'm cheesed off!

HAUNTED.*

My Perrier Award flew across my lounge and smashed into
my framed poster of Eddie Howe.
Oh *great*.
So now my flat was haunted.
This was all I fucking needed.
I plodded into my kitchen.
You've guessed it: slime coating *everything* and some headless
twat sat on top of the dishwasher.
"You a ghost then?" I enquired.
Various bats hanging from above.
Blood oozing out of the fridge.
A mad goblin thing jacking off in the corner.

MY SPECIAL DAY. *

It was my birthday.
I went to the bakery and made a fool of myself,
by and large.
I ordered five doughnuts and stuffed 'em all in
right there on the floor.
Staff started calling me "Sir" a lot and trying
to clear me out.
I waved my passport at their throats.
I jabbed my thumb at the relevant date.
I didn't need them to sing for me, but for
fuck's sake, let me do my doughnut stuff on
my special day!

---

* **JUNIPER:** Do you know the one I like of yours?
  KEY: Well, let's focus on this one, can we?
  JUNIPER: Do you remember you used to do one about an ant or a bee or
       something?
  KEY: Why are we talking about poems that aren't in the book, Em?
  JUNIPER: I wish I could remember the ant one!
  KEY: Who cares about the bloody ant one, Em?!
  JUNIPER: He was drinking cider!
  KEY: Oh, right. Yeah, I mean he was carrying it, but yeah.
  JUNIPER: That was good, all that stuff.
  KEY: "All that stuff". What the hell is "all that stuff"?

LTN – PRG.

I couldn't find my suitcase, so I had to carry
everything loose to Prague.
It was chaos, more or less.
Me with armfuls of clothes and chargers in
Luton airport, trying to persuade them to put
my fleece in the hold.
Organised travellers with suitcases, picking up
my fallen washbags and Grishams and putting
them back on top of my stack.
More or less every single member of staff
bollocking me or telling me to get a bag for
life or asking me why I'd decided to devote a
whole hand to carrying my piping hot Pret
black Americano.

KARATE.*

I shall-I-be-mothered a stack of poppadums and the shards went fucking everywhere.

There was a clean-up operation.

Eventually normal service was resumed and another stack of poppadums was brought out.

I knew I was going to shall-I-be-mother this batch, too, couldn't resist it.

I obliterated the stack with my wicked palm and snorted like an ape.

I noted that one fast-travelling shard had gone a good distance and landed in my Chicken Xacuti, which was being pushed towards me on a trolley-cum-hot plate.

The waiter frowned and his tunic stiffened.

He radioed for the brush and a further tower of intact poppadums.

I was smiling, glugging Kingfisher, stretching my fingers out.

---

*JUNIPER: What's "shall-I-be-mothering" when it's at home?
KEY: Putting my hand through the poppadums.
JUNIPER: Oh. Slapping the poppadums?
KEY: Chopping.
JUNIPER: Karate chop?
KEY: "Shall-I-be-mother".
JUNIPER: Is that what you do to poppadums, then?
KEY: Apparently so, Em.
JUNIPER: You didn't do that when you took me to Monsoon.
KEY: That was before I started doing it.
JUNIPER: This is a new thing?
KEY: 2018, I started.

TODD.*

It was transfer deadline day.
I decided to buy Todd Cantwell from Norwich.
I sold my flat and my breadmaker and my
House of Games carry-on suitcase and had
just about enough to get him on loan.
He arrived at my parents' house and we
wandered through into the garden.
He was sulking and I asked him what was up.
Father came through with cordial and custard
creams, and took photos.
"What's wrong, Todd?" I enquired again.
He asked if I had a football, and I went and
had a look in the shed.

---

*JUNIPER: What's transfer deadline day?
   KEY: What do you think it is?
   JUNIPER: Football?
   KEY: And this is about buying one of the players on transfer deadline day.
   JUNIPER: Can you do that?
   KEY: It's mainly football clubs who do it, to be honest.
   JUNIPER: So someone can't just buy someone for themselves? Like buying a
      billy goat.
   KEY: It would be nuts if someone did. Hang on, what billy goat?
   JUNIPER: So you're telling me you didn't do this?
   KEY: No, Todd stayed at Norwich.
   JUNIPER: To fight for his place.
   KEY: Exactly, Em. Todd Cantwell stayed at Norwich to fight for his place.
   JUNIPER: Sweet.
   KEY: And eventually went to Rangers.

CLOSED.

My fave café was closed.
I went to the one down the road and ordered
a black coffee and an egg to take away.
I was weeping as I walked back to my café.
Why'd they have to shut it?!
I sat outside in the drizzle.
I must admit I pounded my back against the
metal shutters thing.
The street barely seemed to brighten as
dawn took hold.
I groaned and growled as I peeled my egg.

THE ELIZABETH LINE.*

I queued for approx. thirty-five hours.
I have to say it absolutely flew by.
I had plenty of eggs and juice and kept my spirits up by
imagining the end game: gawping at the wood and winking
at the weird guardsmen chappies.
Once I'd shuffled past Her Nibs's boxed-up bod I *fucking
sprinted* to the back of the line again.
I wanted another go!
The queue ended somewhere in Stevenage now.
That's where Lewis Hamilton was born and lived as a child.
He's another one I like.

---

*JUNIPER: Did you really queue for a gawp?
 KEY: Naw.
 JUNIPER: You know the queue I'd have joined?
 KEY: Go on?
 JUNIPER: A queue to give Her a bloody big hug on Her seventieth.
 KEY: Okay.
 JUNIPER: Her on a plinth or some such –
 KEY: Yeah I get the idea, I reckon.
 JUNIPER: The great unwashed giving Her a big old cuddle while she was still
  going great guns.
 KEY: *You'd* have queued, huh?
 JUNIPER: Round the block.

*JUNIPER: Another one.
  KEY: That's the last one.
  JUNIPER: So just the two Hallowe'en poems in September in the end.
  KEY: My shower started firing out urine one Hallowe'en, Em.
  JUNIPER: I honestly don't want to know, Tim.

AN ORANGE GUY.*

I bought a decent-sized pumpkin from the weird guy at the
farm shop.
I made some incisions with my John Lewis knife.
Once I'd built the mouth it snapped shut, biting off my fingers.
I reeled away!
"Now hang on a second!"
My pumpkin had eyes, too – courtesy of yours truly – and
they blinked and squinted.
"Build me legs!"
Great, the beast was talking now.
"Build me some fucking legs!"
I knew what this lad's plan was – me building him legs and
then him chasing me round the kitchen calling me every
name under the sun.
"I will not, sir! No legs for you, old dear!"
He spat his seeds at me with great velocity.
"Legs now, cunt!"
"Not on your nelly!" I was eating mouthfuls of the flesh I'd
harvested from this maniac's skull.
Trying to get a foothold in the argument.
Trying to show this agitated fruit who was boss.

JUNIPER: Two gin and peppermints, please, sir!

KEY: Two? Why you getting two?

JUNIPER: 'Cos I am.

KEY: Hey. Em. What's happening? Look at me.

JUNIPER: You can order two Beck's Viers, if you like.

KEY: I don't want two, Em. I'm just interested to know what's driven you to order two g & p's.

JUNIPER: Well, why d'ya think?

KEY: Well, if I was a betting man –

JUNIPER: "Chapter Ten!" That's why! "Chapter Ten!"

KEY: Oh.

JUNIPER: Should be "October".

KEY: Right.

JUNIPER: So, I'm peed off.

KEY: Erm… I'll get two Beck's Viers, please. And do you have any pan-roasted corn kernels?

JUNIPER: Why would he have pan-roasted corn kernels?

KEY: Good point, just the Viers, please.

JUNIPER: And the g & p's.

KEY: And the g & p's, yes. Thank you, sir.

JUNIPER: Well, don't salute him.

KEY: Bugger me. Can't click him, can't salute him.

JUNIPER: Thank you, sir! Chapter bloody ten, then. Let's go. Come on. Let's get it over with.

KEY: The despair in your eyes, Em.

JUNIPER: That's just my eyes.

KEY: You shouldn't pull this array of faces just because someone hasn't called a chapter "October". I honestly mean that, Em.

JUNIPER: So, tell me, what happens in this chapter then?

KEY: Oh, you know. All sorts.

JUNIPER: So just like all the other chapters then?

KEY: Oh! I go to Paris, that's what happens.

JUNIPER: And when did you go to Paris in real life?

KEY: *Gay Paris.*

JUNIPER: I know, but… when?

KEY: Who cares. Autumn.

JUNIPER: October?

KEY: Chapter Ten.

JUNIPER: Oh just pass 'em here, will ya? Let's have a look at them.

CHAPTER TEN.*

Chapter Ten

B.Y.O.F.

I went up the pub with *a fair amount* of my own furniture.
I sat on my sofa, popped my pint on my crate, plugged my standard lamp in.
Barkeep wandered over.
He said some terrible stuff about how they already had furniture and don't bring my stuff in.
I opened my fridge and took out my parmesan.
He was still talking I reckon, but now I was eating chunks of this hard-ass cheese; listening to my records.
"Come on, sir – this isn't cool."
I'd plugged my leaf-blower in now and started swinging it at the guy.
He was blasted back against the piano by the force of it.
"Get your fat bum off my piano!" I bawled.

Chapter Ten

OPEN WIDE.*

I matched with my dentist on an app.

Uh-oh, basically.

I'd skipped three appointments and I wondered if she'd maybe spotted plaque on my profile.

Either way, it was a time for cool heads.

I brushed my gnashers to within an inch of their lives and waddled to the agreed tapas bar.

She looked lovely without her mask, and her assistant was good craic too, once he'd had a couple.

We retired to a dark recess full of deep-red candles and chilled Spanish beats and my heart raced as my dentist's eyes drifted to my lips.

But then her fingers started prising them open and her assistant started reaching into his rucksack for tools, which glinted in the rancid candlelight.

My date kicked a lever and my chair flew back.

And now her mask was on, and a drill was being plugged in and she was calling me Mr Key and smiling with her eyes.

Anyway, that's what happened.

---

*JUNIPER: Never happened. Bollocks.
  KEY: It *happened* as in *I imagined it.*
  JUNIPER: Right.
  KEY: In October.
  JUNIPER: So, you haven't seen your dentist without her mask on?
  KEY: My head would explode, Em.

FRENCHIE.*

The only thing for it was to go to Paris.

I packed my comb and a Penguin Classic and boarded the Eurostar.

It torpedoed under the Channel as the good Lord intended and soon I had a chocolate éclair hanging out of my mouth and a thin cigarette in my claw.

The air was thick with the French lingo and occasionally I'd get swept away by it, yell something that, to my ear, at any rate, sounded French.

The locals angled their plastic chairs away from me and ultimately I tired of the bistro and hailed the garçon.

I slapped down my euros and trundled down the hill.

I asked assorted Parisians where their damn tower was.

I made myself understood by creating the shape of the bloody great thing with my hands.

---

*JUNIPER: I phoned you when you were in Paris!
  KEY: I was walking up the steps to Montmartre, Em.
  JUNIPER: You had a mad ringtone!
  KEY: 'Cos I was abroad, Em.
  JUNIPER: I thought it was 'cos you were a celeb.
  KEY: Eh?
  JUNIPER: Well, I didn't know you were in Paris, did I?
  KEY: Celebs don't have special ringtones, you know.
  JUNIPER: I thought it might be like the blue tick, I don't know what I'm
      thinking half the time.
  KEY: I had a *croque monsieur* on one of those buses that goes around the
      different sights.
  JUNIPER: Ha ha. Very classy.
  KEY: Some went down my top as we went past the big cathedral thing.

THE SCATTER.

London had all the best stuff and that wasn't right.
The government decreed that London Zoo should be *split up*
and the animals would be *shared around*.
The trucks came and off the animals went.
They got dispersed, basically.
Derby got a hippo.
Keswick, up in the Lake District, got a flamingo and a moth.
Andy Burnham was a pushy old sod and got Manchester a
lion, a panther and five yaks.
Even far-flung villages got at least a snake or a spider.
Eastbourne got a goat in the end.
All that was left in London was a crocodile and a penguin.
They housed these together and turned the rest into a skate
park and a community centre.
Kate from William and Kate came down and reopened the site.
She wore a baseball cap that read "UK People's Zoo Project",
but other than that she looked as lush and glamorous as she
always does.

Chapter Ten

THE 18ᵀᴴ ARRONDISSEMENT. *

I arrived at Montmartre, the famous zone in Paris.
It was very romantic and pissing down with rain and there
was a mad generator thing on the cobbles.
I zipped up my raincoat and did a bit of my "*ou est
McDonald's*" stuff with the locals.
Soon I had the dialogue from Pulp Fiction swilling about in
my ears and strawberry milkshake gushing through my pipes.
My plastic bucket chair creaked as I lowered my face into
what I had somehow ordered.
I think I must have misremembered the word for two.
I certainly had twelve Big Macs in front of me.
With each one I devoured, the prospect of me "prancing
round the Louvre" seemed to become less and less likely.

---

*JUNIPER: Gawd.
  KEY: What?
  JUNIPER: I'd love to go to Paris again. I'd die.
  KEY: Paris doesn't piddle about.
  JUNIPER: Not been for years.
  KEY: It don't change, Em.
  JUNIPER: Honestly think I've been to Lowestoft more than I've been to Paris.
  KEY: *C'est la vie.*
  JUNIPER: I'll take your word for it.
  KEY: I'll take you to Paris, Em.
  JUNIPER: Don't even joke about it.
  KEY: *(Very serious)* Em.
  JUNIPER: Yeah?
  KEY: I wouldn't joke about taking designers to Paris.
  JUNIPER: I love it there, Tim.

---

* KEY: The face, Em.

  JUNIPER: Why isn't this one in the Canterbury chapter?

  KEY: Erm… can't think.

  JUNIPER: It's nuts having a whole Kent chapter and then this one's sat in
        Chapter Ten like a plum.

  KEY: It's about Margate, babe. Ain't nothing in there about Canterbury
        whatsoever.

  JUNIPER: It's, what? Ten mins away from Canterbury?

  KEY: In poetry, that's a lifetime.

THE KENTISH WAY.*

I went to Margate in the end.

I got off the plane and went straight to the arcade.

I threw my two p's into the chute bit and got control of the weird claw thing.

I left that arcade with five tubes of Oreos and headed to my Airbnb on the cliff.

I picked up some Loyd Grossman tomato and basil sauce *en route* and incorporated that with the Oreos and some lasagne sheets to make a *very simple pasta dish.*

I slithered into a tracksuit top and hit the craft beer establishments on the sea front.

Before I knew where I was my body contained four pints of a local beer which had a cartoon pirate on its label.

I talked freely about my projects to the other creatives, and listened to their tales of Kent and film-making.

Beyond that, all I remember is that there was a ship's steering wheel on the wall above the quiz machine.

And, also, that one man's moustache was so long he had to angle his head to get through the toilet door in the same way that people in movies have to angle their planes when they fly into barns.

PORCINE.[*]

I drank some weird bacon drink.
It was, it almost goes without saying, rank.
Worse, I noticed my skin becoming rough and pink and a
cute little tail was spiralling out of my ass.
I felt my nose, but because my hands were also hard, gnarled
trotters, I couldn't work out if it was a snout yet.
I started oinking wildly, smashing into other diners, generally
letting myself down.
I needed someone to find me a mirror!
I needed to check if my damn face had also pigged up!

---

*JUNIPER: Like Heart of a Dog.
KEY: I dunno.
JUNIPER: Or Metamorphosis. He turns into a how's-your-father in that.
KEY: Em, if I'm not allowed to have folk turning into stuff in my poems,
    what's the point in any of it?
JUNIPER: I might write one about a lady who turns into a seagull.
KEY: And you'd be very welcome to, Em.
JUNIPER: Goes back and terrorises her ex-husband.
KEY: Fine, and I'll design it for you in Word.
JUNIPER: Swoops down, nicks his fish and chips.
KEY: Wait a second, what the hell has he done to deserve that?
JUNIPER: You'll have to read it.
KEY: I'd love to, Em. I'm intrigued to know what this poor lad's done to this
    woman that she's getting her gull on and making off with his cod.

I'M YOUR NICK.

It was audition day for The Crown.
I marched in and let them know I was there to play the young Nicholas Witchell.
The casting director said she wasn't sure he'd be featured in the show.
"He's the Royal Correspondent, has been for donkey's," I reminded her, "He'd have been on the scene, they couldn't move for him."
She leafed through the scripts and her assistant googled Witchell.
They glanced up at me and I could tell they were considering my build.
"I can lose two stone like that." I clicked my fingers.
They were scrutinising him, squinting at his locks now.
"If he's in the show —"
"He'll be in the show, he'll be in the show!" I fog-horned.
"We might look for a more ginger-haired artiste."
Now we were all gathered round this image of Witchell.
I peered at his face.
I could play this cunt, I just knew I could.
"Freckle me up, roll me out," I said, "I'm your Witchell, I swear to God."

EARS.*

The couple in the café were having a private conversation.

I was having to *really* strain to hear it.

I was edging towards them, my vast wing almost enveloping them.

Something about Terry? Terry not being straight with the guy? Something to do with a car?

I pulled them both to my end of the table and draped my vast coat over them.

And now we were all under my coat and I could hear *everything*.

"Keep talking," I whispered, "I'm *all* ears."

---

*JUNIPER: Leave them be, surely.
  KEY: I'm terrible for eavesdropping, Em. I really am.
  JUNIPER: It's rude, that's my honest opinion.
  KEY: I've been known to thank people as I leave.
  JUNIPER: Thank them? Jesus.
  KEY: They don't know why I'm thanking them.
  JUNIPER: Well, why would they?
  KEY: Daft sods. They don't know what the hell's going on.

LISTE DE CHOSES À FAIRE AVANT DE MOURIR.*

I unfurled my bucket list.
I was interested to see if any of my dreams were based in Paris.
Yes!
"Take off trousers, jump in Seine."
Okey doke – that one was *crying out* to be done in Paris.
I unbuckled my jeans and let the denim fall.
I left my Airbnb and made my way to the Métro.
Parisians pointed at my Homer Simpson underpants and laughed like drains.
They thought I was crackers.
I nodded along, barely looked up from my Penguin Classic edition of Robinson Crusoe as the train rattled along.
These people didn't even know what the next part of my plan was.

＊JUNIPER: Would you ever live abroad, do you think?
KEY: Who, me?
JUNIPER: You like your little trips.
KEY: Oh, yeah.
JUNIPER: Relocate to Copenhagen, see who salutes.
KEY: I'd maybe live in The States, as they call them.
JUNIPER: Yes! Like Dawn from The Office.
KEY: No language barrier, I love the music out there, you know.
JUNIPER: Big portions.
KEY: Eh?
JUNIPER: No, as in, they pile it high. That's all.
KEY: I'm not going there to eat, Em.
JUNIPER: They'll mix a candy bar into a meatball sauce if you ask 'em.
KEY: Why am I asking 'em though, Em? Seriously. Jeez Louise.

*JUNIPER: You know what I'm thinking?

KEY: You're thinking another walk? You're thinking we press your man for details on the charcuterie board? You're thinking you're having a nice time? You're thinking you're loving the project?

JUNIPER: I'm thinking what's the title?

KEY: Huh? What title?

JUNIPER: Of the book.

KEY: Just like... "Here it is". Yer know. "Our book".

JUNIPER: You haven't had *thoughts*?

KEY: Oh. Dunno. "Canterbury" maybe. "Reflections on –"

JUNIPER: You know what I think you should call it?

KEY: Go on. I'm on hooks.

JUNIPER: I'm thinking you call it "Chapters".

KEY: Yeah.

JUNIPER: Because your chapters are such a disgrace.

KEY: Yeah.

JUNIPER: Well, stop saying yeah. I'm serious.

KEY: Yeah, I think I'll do that.

JUNIPER: Oh. Really?

KEY: Yeah.

JUNIPER: You've got your Sharpie out.

KEY: Easiest decision I've ever made.

JUNIPER: Ha.

KEY: There's still three more and we'll probably fall out about all three. So, yeah. "Chapters".

JUNIPER: 'Cos, look. This one's "November and December". So it goes: "September", then "Ten", then "November and December". I mean, it's a disgrace.

KEY: It's inexcusable, Em.

JUNIPER: In my opinion, yeah.

KEY: Well, it's called "Chapters" now.

JUNIPER: Owning it.

KEY: Holding my hands up. "I fucked up the chapters, now my book's called 'Chapters'. Sorry everyone."

JUNIPER: Gimme these ones then.

KEY: "November and December". Back to months. You like it when it's months.

JUNIPER: Is it set in November and December?

KEY: Well, you'd certainly think so, Em. That's what the title would suggest.

NOVEMBER AND DECEMBER.*

SNOWY.

Snow fell.
It was glorious.
Really beautiful.
Like icing sugar had been dropped from the heavens.
It smelled like icing sugar, too.
I took a handful off a car and licked it.
What the hell!?
It *was* icing sugar!
What the fuck was the dopey cunt up to now?
Why the hell had he covered the city in icing sugar?
I ate another pawful and grimaced.
How much had this cost even?

PIGGIE.*

Someone had brought a pig to the pub.
"Here piggie, piggie!"
I was lashed, I wanted him near me.
I wanted to wrap my scarf around his
thick neck.
What I wanted more than anything else
was to create the impression that I was
with the pig.

***JUNIPER:** Ha!
  KEY: What?
  JUNIPER: Someone's finally lost it.
  KEY: Meaning what?
  JUNIPER: This one's already been in.
  KEY: Uh-huh.
  JUNIPER: In one of the other chapters.
  KEY: Well, I'm not apologising for that. I love this one.
  JUNIPER: Are you actually joking?
  KEY: Do I look like I'm joking?
  JUNIPER: As in, what, you're having it in twice?
  KEY: Well, I think three times would be taking the piss, put it that way.
  JUNIPER: What kind of a poet puts the same unit in twice?
  KEY: You're looking at him, babe.
  JUNIPER: Oh. My. God. Double poem!
  KEY: Ha ha! In a good way, Em. Always remember that.
    In a good way.

THE METEOR STRIKE.

Buddy hopped on the 134.
There was a big unit on there.
"Hello, I'm Fatberg."
Buddy was smitten.
She bowed her head as Fatberg smiled and
joked and played the fool.
The bus slowed; it was bulging with
electricity.
"This is my stop, Mr Fatberg."
Fatberg's heart was racing.
"Will you marry me?"
Buddy bit her lip.
"Sure."

THE GIRL WITH THE YELLOW COAT.

I helped the girl with the yellow coat
up into the tree.
Then I joined her.
We sat up there like two owls.
Drinking Amstel.
Waiting for dawn to break.

NATURE'S SYRUP.

Mr Lewis drilled into a tree and sucked nine
litres of sap out.
He carried it back to Frances.
"Guess what's in my bag, Fran?"
"Donkey crap, knowing you."
Mr Lewis split the bag with a peach knife and
drained the sap into a pan.
He began heating the sap.
Frances smiled as the caramel scent filled the
kitchen.
She knew that they would feed it to one another
once it was warm.
She knew that Mr Lewis would drizzle it on
her breasts.
She knew that it would make her feel
beautiful, desired.

PLAGUE.*

I opened the door to the lounge.

Fuck. Me.

I couldn't believe what I was looking at.

There were approx. eighty Santas in there.

Place was crawling with 'em.

Two on the beanbag, six crammed onto the
sofa, and the rest just sort of everywhere,
stacked, slumped, writhing.

It was obscene!

It looked like a goddamn Caravaggio painting
if that's the chap I'm thinking of.

It's an obvious point but I had never seen so
many Santas.

Some were groaning; the room fucking stunk.

Then: a thud.

Another Santa crawling out from the fireplace.

Oh Christ.

They were still coming.

*JUNIPER: Room full of Santas now?
  KEY: Ha ha. I know, fuck tons of 'em everywhere.
JUNIPER: So why d'ya have to put this one in?
  KEY: I didn't have to, Em. Chose to. Went for it.
JUNIPER: It's enough to put you off Christmas forever.
  KEY: Ha ha. Big pile of Santas! Worst-case scenario. Merry Christmas, Em!
JUNIPER: I won't be able to sleep, I don't think.
  KEY: Christmas design?
JUNIPER: Yeah. Course.

FULLY FORMED.

Colette gave birth to an adult.
She was devastated.
She'd bought cots and stuff.
Lionel was in his late thirties.
He kept talking about the Bros
documentary and going travelling.

*JUNIPER: I mean, really?

KEY: I know. Footy chapter. Out of nowhere.

JUNIPER: Whole chapter about footy?

KEY: And yet you wouldn't bat an eyelid if I put one in about Wimbledon.

JUNIPER: Because tennis is for everyone. Footy's for yobs.

KEY: We've been through this, Em. *Judi Dench* watches the footy. *Jessica Ennis-Hill* watches the footy. But why let the facts get in the way of a good story.

JUNIPER: So you just drop everything, do a whole chapter about footy, half your bloody readers' eyes glazing over, the other half cracking open the Holsten Pils, jacking off, chanting about Sven-Göran Eriksson.

KEY: What the fuck?

JUNIPER: You got eight pages of this stuff, look.

KEY: Keira Knightley watches the footy, Em.

JUNIPER: Who wants to read about this drivel?

KEY: She's a massive fuck-off Hammer, Keira is.

JUNIPER: Ha ha. That's interview talk, they say any old thing these people.

KEY: And that's before we even mention Adele.

JUNIPER: Adele's into it, huh?

KEY: Spurs. Learnt to sing on the terraces.

JUNIPER: Adele did?

KEY: So it's not just big old bruising beefcakes with tattoos on their knuckles, Em. I promise you it's not.

JUNIPER: Well, obviously I know it's not quite that simple, no.

KEY: Croatia went deep as fuck again, I see.

JUNIPER: People going about their day, skimming through your poems – good people – and then suddenly a whole chapter dedicated to the *wonderful* Qataris and their *magnificent* football tournament in the depths of the desert.

KEY: It's four poems, Em. *Four*. Who gives a fuck? I'm serious.

JUNIPER: Okay, hand it over. And can we please get these things filled up?

KEY: Sir!

JUNIPER: Sir! We're gasping over here! Sir!

KEY: Did you watch any of it?

JUNIPER: The final, yeah.

KEY: You see?

JUNIPER: And a couple of the quarters, some last sixteen stuff and most of the group stages.

KEY: Excuse me?

THE 2022 FIFA WORLD CUP, DOHA.*

*JUNIPER: I'm a bit… worried.

KEY: Worried how?

JUNIPER: Just, if folk are reading this in twenty years' time?

KEY: I don't understand your point, Em.

JUNIPER: People won't know what you're going on about, that's all. They won't know the World Cup was set at Christmas.

KEY: Staged, Em. It was staged in December. Not "set at Christmas".

JUNIPER: I think the ones I like best could happen at any time.

KEY: My readership are smart, Em. They work shit out. Relax.

JUNIPER: But the ones where it's just like a guy eating a pelican or whatever –

KEY: What?

JUNIPER: But you know what I mean –

KEY: I have no idea, Em. I've never written a single thing about that guy. He sounds gross!

JUNIPER: He's just an example.

KEY: Yeah, and a fucking rancid one and all.

·134·

FIGUREHEAD.*

Santa was way behind with everything because of the bloody World Cup.

Basically, he'd been enlisted by the Qataris to be an ambassador figure.

So, that's all of November and half of December with him over there.

Photo opportunities, him doing keepy-uppies in malls, him saying there's more to Qatar than oil and bad vibes.

They liked it most when they'd cut to him in the stands.

He'd wave a thick red mitten and smile.

The truth of it was he was burning up in his felt tunic.

Rivulets of sweat sloshed through his arse crack.

Partly because of the rancid heat.

Partly because he wasn't 100% sure he should have taken the money.

MOST UNWELCOME.

A hooligan made it to Qatar.
"Hey, I'm a hooligan."
A chap at customs looked over his spectacles at our hero.
"We're not really into the hooligan vibe, I'm afraid."
The hooligan looked sad and fiddled with his flat cap.
"Can't I come in and tear things up though?"
Another Qatari with a marginally bigger moustache
wandered over and shook his head.
The hooligan was in tears.
"Can I come in and sit nicely then?"
A pause.
"Please?"
A close-up of the passport being stamped.
Tears splashing onto the wet ink.

IT MATTERS MORE.*

There was *literally* nothing else for it:
I decided to play a little drinking game for Brazil vs
Switzerland.
Well, I collected what needed to be collected from Londis
and laid it all out.
I would do half a Strongbow for a Brazil goal.
It'd be half a Boddingtons for yours truly if the dear old
Swiss made the net bulge.
A penalty would yield a lovely big glass of scotch, and then
the basics:
Creme Egg for a corner, 50g of Red Leicester for an offside
and a fuckload of glue for *any throw-in*.
I flicked off my trainers and affixed my bib.
Now I was *invested*.

---

* **JUNIPER:** I watched that one.
    KEY: Oh, you did, huh?
    JUNIPER: Swiss couldn't believe their luck, most probably.
    KEY: What luck?
    JUNIPER: Starting line-ups come through: no Neymar.
    KEY: Oh yeah, that.
    JUNIPER: "That"? Swiss are competitive at the best of times. And then no
        Neymar?
    KEY: Yup, big chance for the Swiss.
    JUNIPER: What big chance? You forget Brazil have a certain Mr Casemiro
        pulling the strings, my friend.
    KEY: Well.
    JUNIPER: And who's that I've got on my bench? Oh I see, a little-known
        Arsenal striker by the name of Mr Gabriel Jesus.
    KEY: Hm-hm.
    JUNIPER: 1:0, and on we go.
    KEY: Yup. Yup it was 1:0, that one.

*JUNIPER: Last World Cup one?

   KEY: Jesus wept, Em. Most talked about sporting event in decades and I can't hammer out some gash about it?

JUNIPER: But now we go back to normal?

   KEY: You make it sound like I kidnapped you, Em.

JUNIPER: I was pleased for Messi, anyway.

   KEY: The atomic flea.

JUNIPER: Ha ha! Really? That's his nickname?

   KEY: The atomic flea.

JUNIPER: Oh please write one about that, Tim. Please write a poem about the atomic flea!

   KEY: Thought you wanted me to draw a line under the World Cup ones.

JUNIPER: But one about the atomic flea! Please! With his little goggles!

   KEY: What goggles?

JUNIPER: Zipping around in his Argentina shirt, solving crimes!

   KEY: What the fuck are you going on about, Em?

DOHA IN THE SPRINGTIME.*

I had seen enough.
I booked to go to Qatar in March.
The old sods had won me over.
You can't get the whole vibe through your TV screen of
course, but you get a flavour and what I saw: I liked.
I checked various websites to see whether FIFA would also be
maintaining a presence until spring.
It'd be a shame to fly all that way and not have FIFA looming
ominously in the background throughout my long weekend.

*JUNIPER: "The Dregs" though.

KEY: Why not?

JUNIPER: And the final chapter, too.

KEY: Dreggy wegs!

JUNIPER: If I was in charge of chapters –

KEY: Big if, Em.

JUNIPER: I'd keep it a secret that these ones are dregs.

KEY: It's just a phrase, Em. It's not me saying these ones are garbage.

JUNIPER: People will decide for themselves.

KEY: They're no worse than a lot of what's come before.

JUNIPER: Hey!

KEY: What?

JUNIPER: I think I've had a thought!

KEY: What thought?

JUNIPER: Some people might read this on a plane!

KEY: That is a thought.

JUNIPER: So, someone could get on a plane, order a Heineken and then be reading this.

KEY: Well, that applies to any book, Em.

JUNIPER: I think that's wild. Someone however many miles above the sea just reading this. Waiting for the entertainment to whirr into life.

KEY: Oh.

JUNIPER: What?

KEY: So we're saying it's just while they're waiting for the films to start.

JUNIPER: Oh. I mean, yeah. I think once that's up and running most people tend to go with that.

KEY: Slide their anthologies into the netting bit on the back of the seat in front.

JUNIPER: Ha ha. Slide it back out on the descent.

KEY: Yeah.

JUNIPER: Still, nice knowing there might be some frequent flyer up there flicking through your poems.

KEY: Yeah. Yeah that does sound kind of nice.

JUNIPER: "Kind of nice".

KEY: No. No, that's exciting. Ooh.

JUNIPER: What?

KEY: That noise, with your straw.

JUNIPER: Well, it's 'cos I'm finished.

KEY: Then push your g & p away nicely, Em. That's repulsive.

JUNIPER: There I've pushed it away. Right. Let's look at the dregs then.

THE DREGS.*

*JUNIPER: Is this the one from the photos?

    KEY: Yes, but if you're going to tell me it was a small wheel, I don't want to hear it, Em.

  JUNIPER: It was a pecker.

    KEY: A height's a height, Em. Once it goes over twenty feet all bets are off.

  JUNIPER: Ha ha! You were white as a sheet.

    KEY: You do know you can drown in a centimetre of water, Em. You do *actually* know that?

  JUNIPER: You were strapped in, come on.

    KEY: Thank God.

  JUNIPER: Ha ha! Your niece was pissing herself.

    KEY: Because she's eight, Em. She hasn't got a clue. Wait 'til she's had a bit of experience with heights. Wait 'til she's seen the damage they can cause.

  JUNIPER: Being *looked after* by an eight-year-old!

    KEY: That was the problem, Em. She didn't take control of the situation. That's where the trouble began.

FERRIS.*

I went on the big wheel with my niece.
It went too high and I got scared and had to hold onto the child for reassurance.
She was laughing which didn't help matters and made the seat-bit rock.
I needed her to calm me down, but I'd come to the wrong place, believe me.
She pulled a spanner from her dungarees and kept pretending to undo the nuts.
Also, she jumped down to the seat below, gave the guys down there a right old shock.
I was paralysed with fear up there!
I was yelling at my niece to climb the hell back up the wires.
But I was so petrified the only thing that came out my mouth was a – horrible phrase – panicked rasp.
And that just made her laugh all the more.

ASHES.

I opted to give up cigs in honour of New Year's Eve.
I waddled round my flat, locating all the horrible fags from all my battered packets.
These needed to be smoked before the big night.
I opened my rum and inhaled the offending stack.
A final bonfire of evil before knocking it on the head forever.
There were still a handful left and I took them to the boozer to smoke before the countdown.
Happy New Year.
I must admit, I had a few left at midnight and, forgive me, I smoked these after the gong.
I even ran across the road in the wee hours, snuck a packet under the radar before dawn.
The rum tasted good as the sun came up, but I knew jet-black coffee would be best.
I staggered out onto the street, my lighter burning the chill mist, turning the tip of my Rothmans orange.
I struck out for Soho.
New beginnings.
I'd smoke a handful outside Le Pain Quotidien before heading inside for my omelette.

SIR NICK.*

A new series of *I'm A Celebrity*, and Pret started doing
kangaroo's penises.

It was, of course, a mad publicity stunt.

But soon celebs started coming down.

Trying to prove themselves, trying to show how ideal they'd
be in the jungle.

Jenas, Faldo, Nancy Sinatra.

They all came down.

Washing their penises down with orange juices or ginger beer.

Faldo *demanding* they put cum in his coffee – winking at the
CCTV cameras.

---

*JUNIPER: Would you go on?
  KEY: I'm a celebrity?
  JUNIPER: I know, that's why I'm asking.
  KEY: Naw. Wouldn't go on. I struggle to eat blue cheese, no way I'm getting an
    anus down.
  JUNIPER: You'd meet Ant and Dec.
  KEY: Yeah, I'd meet them about three times for about one minute a time.
    Not worth it.
  JUNIPER: You've done House of Games.
  KEY: That's light ents, Em.
  JUNIPER: Oh, okay.
  KEY: If you think House of Games is reality TV you're fucking nuts.

I'M TIMING YER.*

My wife started wearing a stopwatch round her neck.

"Ignore this," she said.

That only made me look at it more.

She seemed to be starting it every time I started speaking and stopping it when I'd finished.

"Rosemary, the stopwatch –"

"I thought we were ignoring the stopwatch, Kenneth."

"I know, just –" She started it again.

"I'm trying to ignore it, Ro, honestly I am…"

I ran out of words, slumped down, clutched my knees.

She pressed stop.

---

*JUNIPER: Do you worry that you talk too much?
KEY: Excuse me?
JUNIPER: No, just as in, do you wonder, yeah, if you talk too much?
KEY: *No I do not.* What the actual fuck?
JUNIPER: Well, I don't know. They come from *somewhere*, don't they?
KEY: I barely say anything, Em. Honestly I don't.
JUNIPER: Well, I'm here if you ever want to talk about it.
KEY: "It"? What the fuck is going on here, Em?
JUNIPER: Oh I don't know. Ignore me, I'm drunk.
KEY: On nine gin and peppermints? I don't believe it for a minute.
JUNIPER: No, not drunk, tired then. I don't know. Come on, next poem.
KEY: What the hell's happening here, Em? Talk about *what?*

BUENOS AIRES.*

Gumposs hurtled out of the bank, peeling off
his balaclava as he ran.
His half-open Adidas holdall belched out
bills as he clattered down the road.
His ass honked out guffs into the afternoon
sunshine, then:
Wham!
A tiny paw gripping his loathsome collar, his
body flung hard into the garbage cans.
The atomic flea stood at his feet now, his
pale blue and white football jersey slick to his
abdomen.
The robber looked up miserably.
"Olá." The atomic flea slung off his goggles.
He shook out his hair.
He stood in the dust.
"Hand over the holdall and shut the fuck
up," he rasped.

*JUNIPER: Yay!

*JUNIPER: The last poem.

  KEY: Yup.

  JUNIPER: We got there.

  KEY: We always do, Em.

  JUNIPER: Well, there we are. All very interesting.

  KEY: "Interesting"?

  JUNIPER: Well, it is interesting, going through them all.

  KEY: Never tell a poet his anthology is "interesting", Em.

  JUNIPER: Or her.

  KEY: Well, anyway. Those are the poems.

  JUNIPER: And now off I pop.

  KEY: "The design phase".

  JUNIPER: I'll make them look lush.

  KEY: And then we reconvene.

  JUNIPER: Where?

  KEY: Neutral territory.

  JUNIPER: Ooh!

  KEY: And you'll have designed them and it will be a great day.

  JUNIPER: Let's go abroad!

  KEY: I'm ruling nothing out, Em. Nothing.

  JUNIPER: Right. Drinks… Sir!

  KEY: Now who's clicking her fingers?

  JUNIPER: I'm clicking the lot! I'm fucking pumped.

BULBOUS.*

I picked up an eye-catching root vegetable in the
greengrocer's in town.
Its shape was rude, as in *rude*.
As in it resembled a decent-sized penis and had the gonads to
back it up.
I giggled tons, but then saw the cashier gawping at me and I
went bright red and stuffed the piece down my trousers.
Around 45 mins later I'm getting patted down by two
security guards in the office bit out back.
When the thinner of the two hauled it out of my drawers
and slapped it on the table I went that red colour again but
then they got the giggles and soon the three off us were all
wetting ourselves, miming that it was our penis, *et cetera*.
It was such a rude shape and such a great day.

DOTTING THE I's.

The sound of piping hot water running through an old-fashioned tap, bubbles thickening, the mild scent of a cherry vanilla candle skimming against the tiles. And, barely visible through the steam: a phone call.

KEY: Well, have you got a pen?

JUNIPER: You're in luck, I have my calligraphy pen.

KEY: And an Eccles cake in your mouth, by the sounds of it.

JUNIPER: It's Sunday night. I'm luxuriating.

KEY: You're in the tub, huh?

JUNIPER: What am I writing down, anyway?

KEY: Oh. You have paper in there?

JUNIPER: I'll scribble on the tiles, type it up after.

KEY: Oh, okay. So, Phoebe, Dan, Peter, LK. The usual, basically.

JUNIPER: Oh, I see. *The acknowledgments.*

KEY: They must feel seen, Em. These people *have* to be recognised.

JUNIPER: Yuh. The final piece of the jigsaw.

KEY: Yes! Apart from the index.

JUNIPER: Please don't send me an index, Tim.

KEY: And then it'll be a case of *bosh*. CTRL + P, and see you on the other side.

JUNIPER: What other side?

KEY: Or should I say *"L'autre side"*. I've booked something for us, Em.

JUNIPER: Oh, stop talking in riddles, can't you?

KEY: Okay, so... Sweetie Pie and Breeno. Buddy, of course –

JUNIPER: Back to the acknowledgments...

KEY: These people read it, Em. They sat through the poems. They *must* feel seen.

JUNIPER: I read the poems too!

KEY: You're top of my list, Em. I'm finishing with you.

JUNIPER: Oh God, no, I didn't mean that. I loved the poems. I don't want acknowledging.

KEY: You need to be acknowledged to within an inch of your life, Em.

JUNIPER: You haven't seen my design yet!

KEY: I'm sure I'll *purr*, Em.

JUNIPER: I'm doing little illustrations this time.

KEY: Big letters: EMILY JUNIPER. You need your own tile.

JUNIPER: Oh don't. It's embarrassing.

KEY: You must feel seen.

JUNIPER: I do. I do feel seen. Now, can I focus on my bath?

KEY: I want your name plastered all over this book, Em.

JUNIPER: I'll scribble it in some margin somewhere, I'm sure.

KEY: Then Calverts. The printers. CBL, God love 'em. And then any of your mob?

JUNIPER: Katie! The linchpin.

KEY: What the fuck is a linchpin?

JUNIPER: And Tom! He's been a stalwart, to be fair.

KEY: Yah! Bung him down.

JUNIPER: And then let me bathe?

KEY: Yes! Of course. Bathe! You get your hippo on.

JUNIPER: And then type it up. And then –

KEY: And then *un petit au revoir.* And then *un rendezvous magnifique!*

JUNIPER: Riddles again!

KEY: Tatty bye, Em!!!!

INDEX BY WHAT'S GOING ON IN THE POEMS.

Kicking The Pelican Brief along outside Dixons or whatever it is now. *(pg 99.)*

Legend goes out on the lash the night before, can't get the job done. *(pg 20.)*

Lying to get out of milking dirty great cows. *(pg 15.)*

Making the best of it and canoodling with a spiky little so-and-so. *(pg 91.)*

A **meditation** on the power and the beauty of snowfall. *(pg 125.)*

New take on the chap in the Bible who can't help checking himself out every two seconds. *(pg 11.)*

The **nuts** and bolts of landing something juicy in the DC Universe. *(pg 44.)*

On the **unforgiving** underfoot conditions of Kent's famous UNESCO World Heritage Site. *(pg 29.)*

Overcooking your diary, not cancelling shit, giving it all a decent stir, seeing who salutes. *(pg 40.)*

The **perils** of being on a date with a casting director. *(pg 89.)*

The **perils** of parking your refrigerator right next to your kettle. *(pg 45.)*

Piecing things together upon discovering an abnormality on the stepograph. *(pg 43.)*

Piss-take slaphead sneering at the flab. *(pg 16.)*

Pitching up to a date forty minutes late and with an exposed socket. *(pg 87.)*

A **poetical** tribute to a niece's scandalous behaviour on a wheel. *(pg 143.)*

Pulling up a seat and driving a grizzly oak stake through some poor lovebirds' evening. *(pg 51.)*

Putting a sneaky offer in for a willowy Number Ten, with the clocks running down. *(pg 101.)*

A **rebuilding** exercise after the early loss of Zak Crawley. *(pg 75.)*

Regressing to an inferior beast on account of quantity of sun on the back. *(pg 73.)*

The **rewards** that come when you give the bell a decent whack in The Garden of England. *(pg 30.)*

Sausage fingers hits the wrong button. *(pg 90.)*

A **scary** poem about some dead bloke disturbing my peace and quiet. *(pg 97.)*

Scavenging for shade and cream on the hottest day of the century. *(pg 76.)*

Seamlessly folding a football match into your everyday regime. *(pg 137.)*

Sitting with my dentist above me eight times and then across from me once. *(pg 111.)*

Slathering respect all over the streets of London. *(pg 103.)*

Smacking a dweeb for a freebie down at Pret. *(pg 6.)*

Sniping at the fanbase. *(pg 65.)*

Some kind of glitch and then a confused grown-up staggering into the world. *(pg 131.)*

Someone with the actual iron hazelnuts to change their mind on being presented with new evidence. *(pg 50.)*

Spider sets the trap, Tory politician walks into it. *(pg 7.)*

Stocking up for a trip to deepest Cornwall. *(pg 49.)*

These two people now have a new home, a new car, a baby, and are trying to get a free barbecue. *(pg 127.)*

Thunderclap moment between absent-minded drinker and thickset innkeeper. *(pg 17.)*

Travelling from Durham to London with Rory Stewart burrowing into your ears. *(pg 21.)*

Turning into an aquatic mammal and requiring immediate passage to an ocean or similar. *(pg 47.)*

Two boozehounds engaging in how's-yerfather in some squalid hostelry in the middle of Gawd knows where. *(pg 61.)*

The **types** of things that can happen when you go to Margate or Ramsgate. *(pg 117.)*

The **unalloyed** joy of meeting your soulmate. *(pg 85.)*

The **ups** and downs of drinking with an arsehole. *(pg 3.)*

The **upside** of holding the footy somewhere as strict as fuck. *(pg 136.)*

When it becomes imperative to leave the cakes and liquor and head towards the light. *(pg 144.)*

When it looks snazzy in the shop but it hurts once it's on. *(pg 39.)*

When you have a clock on you and it gets in your head. *(pg 146.)*

Worst-case scenario poetry based on a news story you wouldn't particularly like to come across. *(pg 9.)*

Written in tribute to the hugely talented Kentish Long-Tail and gifted miserabilist. *(pg 38.)*